SCIENCE

UNDERSTANDING YOUR ENVIRONMENT

GEORGE G. MALLINSON
Distinguished Professor
of Science Education
Western Michigan University

JACQUELINE B. MALLINSON
Associate Professor of Science
Western Michigan University

DOUGLAS G. BROWN
Teacher at the Individualized Learning Center
Sioux City, Iowa, Community Schools

JOHN KNAPP II
Associate Professor of Science Education
State University of New York—Oswego

WILLIAM L. SMALLWOOD
Teacher and Former Science Coordinator
Mountain Home, Idaho, Public Schools

SILVER BURDETT COMPANY
Morristown, New Jersey
Glenview, IL • Palo Alto • Dallas • Atlanta

SCIENCE

UNDERSTANDING YOUR ENVIRONMENT

THE SILVER BURDETT ELEMENTARY SCIENCE PROGRAM K–6

PUPILS' BOOKS AND TEACHERS' EDITIONS
LEVELS ONE THROUGH SIX

RECORD BOOKS IN SPIRIT-MASTER FORM
LEVELS THREE THROUGH SIX

AUTHORS:
GEORGE G. MALLINSON
JACQUELINE B. MALLINSON
DOUGLAS G. BROWN
WILLIAM L. SMALLWOOD
JOHN KNAPP II

Critic Readers
Dr. Jean Adenika
University of California
Irvine, California

Richard Codispoti
Director, Science Education
Cleveland Public Schools
Cleveland, Ohio

Luis Antonio Cordova
Colegio Our Lady of Pilar
Hato Rey, Puerto Rico

Sister Marie Savickas, C.S.A.
University of Minnesota
Morris, Minnesota

Jack R. Warren
Science Coordinator
Clayton County Schools
Jonesboro, Georgia

Individualized Extension Activities
Enrichment and Evaluative Materials (pupil
activity sheets on spirit masters)
for Grades 1 and 2
Teachers' Guides

Science Labs
Levels 1–6

Sound Filmstrips
60 filmstrips and cassettes for Levels 1–6

Beginner Series in Science
Multimedia Learning Activity Units with
sound filmstrips

Pictures That Teach—Science
28 charts and Teacher's Manual

Environmental Education Picture Packet
24 pictures and Teacher's Manual

CONTENTS

The Sun and the Planets

In the daytime, you can see only one star. That star is the sun. It looks so big and bright because it is so near. It is thousands of times closer to us than any other star.

The sun is a giant ball of glowing gases. Light shines out from it in all directions. Light is one kind of **energy. (en′ər jē)** Only a tiny bit of this light energy strikes Earth. But without light energy there would be no life on Earth.

Each year Earth circles the sun. Eight other **planets (plan′ itz)** also circle the sun. Two are closer to the sun than Earth is. Six are farther away. Some are larger then Earth. Four are smaller. Many planets have moons that circle them. The sun, the planets, and their moons make up the **solar system (sō′ler sis′təm).**

Every day the sun rises and sets. Here it is setting behind a hill. The sun is our closest star. It is hundreds of times bigger than the earth.

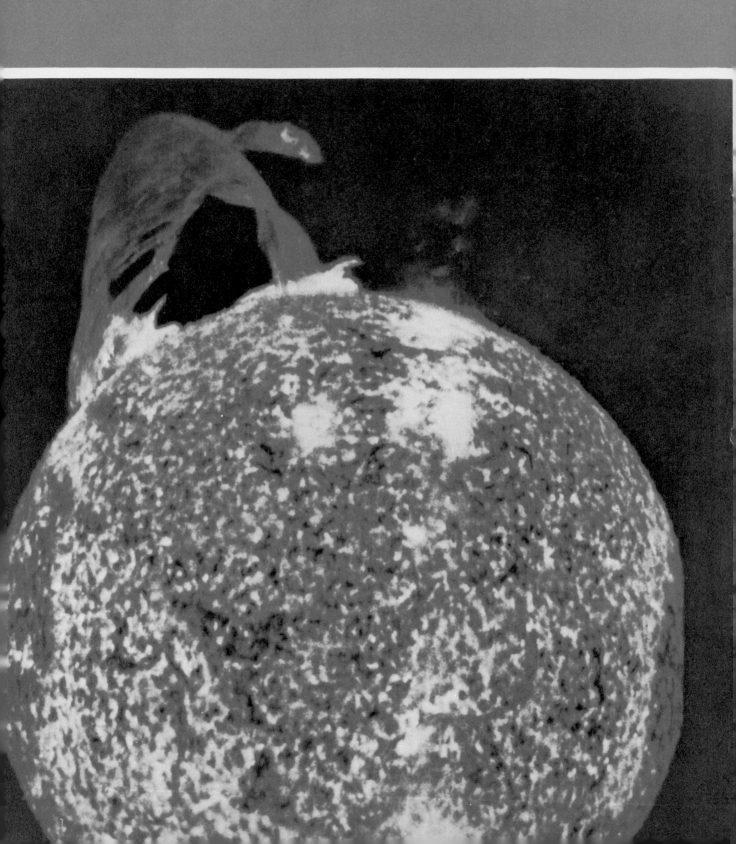

The Sun— An Important Star

The sun is always giving off great amounts of energy. This energy travels out from the sun in all directions. Let's compare this to people crowded around a campfire. Those closest to the fire are the warmest. Those farthest away are the coolest. So, too, those closest to the fire get the most light. Those farthest from the campfire are almost in the dark. Both light and heat are forms of energy. The sun gives off much energy. You can see some of this energy.

The nine planets receive only a small amount of this energy. Planets near the sun get more energy than planets that are farther away.

To you, the sun looks like a very bright, quiet ball in the sky. It is hard to think of it as a roaring ball of fire. It is harder still to think of it as having storms. But often there are great storms on the sun. Sometimes flares shoot out many thousands of kilometers from the sun. You can see one such storm in the picture at the left.

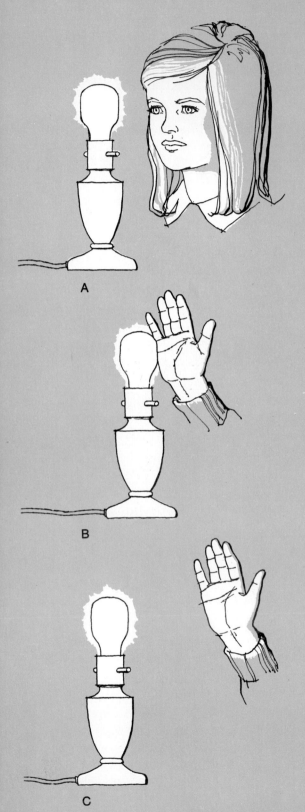

Activity 1

What is radiant energy?

You need:

Lamp with a 100-watt bulb

A. Put the lamp on your desk. Take the shade off the lamp. Turn on the light. Look at the way the light shines.

B. Put your hand a few centimeters from the light bulb. How does your hand feel?

C. Slowly move your hand away from the light. How does your hand feel?

Answer these:

1. In which direction did the light travel from the lamp?

2. How did your hand feel when it was close to the lamp?

3. How did your hand feel as you moved it away from the lamp? Did both sides of your hand feel the same?

4. How is this light like sunlight?

5. Make believe your hand is a planet. Move it around the lamp. What does this tell you about the energy each planet gets?

The sun's energy goes through space in waves. These waves are called **radiant** (rā′dē ənt) **energy.** The waves strike objects in space. A change takes place in the objects they strike. Some of the radiant energy changes to heat. This heat energy raises the **temperature** (tem′ pər ə chər) of the object. If an object loses heat energy, its temperature goes down. A **thermometer** (thər mom′ ə tər) is used to measure temperature.

1. How does the sun's energy travel through space?

2. What is used to measure temperature?

There are many kinds of thermometers. They ·all measure temperature. Which of the thermometers shown here are used in your home?

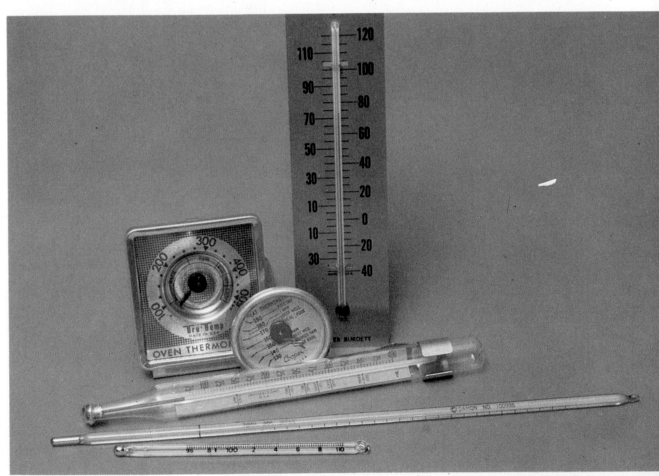

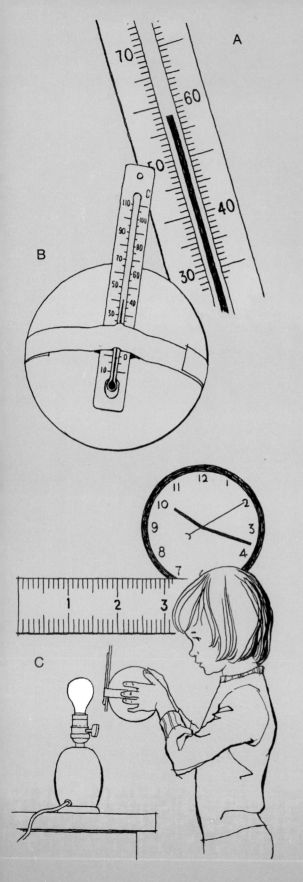

Activity 2

How do we measure changes in temperature?

You need:

Lamp with a 100-watt bulb	a planet)
Thermometer	Metric ruler
Plastic ball (to represent	Masking tape

A. Before you start, make sure you know how to read a thermometer. Check with your teacher if you need help.

B. Tape the thermometer to the ball. Record the temperature on the thermometer.

C. Turn on the lamp. Hold the ball 3 cm from the light bulb. Hold the ball there for 10 seconds. Record the temperature.

D. Take the ball away for about a minute. Now hold the ball 6 cm from the light bulb. Again, hold the ball for 10 seconds. Record the temperature.

E. Do this four more times. Do it at distances of 9, 12, 15, and 18 cm.

Answer these:
1. What was the temperature at each of the distances?
2. What happened to the temperature as you moved the ball?

WHAT DOES ENERGY DO?

Energy from the sun does more than warm our bodies. It warms the sea and the land. Pour just enough water into a baby-food jar to cover the bottom. Set the jar in a window for a day or two. What will happen? The water will **evaporate** (i vap′ ə rāt) and go into the air. Energy from the sun causes water to evaporate.

Large amounts of water evaporate from oceans and lakes. Your school playground dries quickly after a rain shower. The water evaporates. It rises with warm air. Later the air cools. Then the water in the air forms clouds. Still later, it will fall again as rain. Plants use the water in warm, wet soil. Plants also use energy from the sun to grow. People and animals have food because of this radiant energy.

Do other planets have life on them? Scientists do not think so. However, they are not so sure about Mars. In 1976, two Viking spacecraft landed on Mars. They sent back much information. Several experiments were done to see if there was life on Mars. But the results are still not clear.

The other planets seem too hot or too cold to have living things. Some planets may not have materials needed for life.

Many countries have enough water. But the water may be too salty to drink. This water is too salty to drink. The sun's energy is used to take salt from the water.

THE ORBITING PLANETS

All nine planets travel around the sun. The paths they travel are called **orbits** (ôr′ bits). The orbits are like flat circles. Imagine nine marbles rolling around on a dinner plate. The marbles are of different

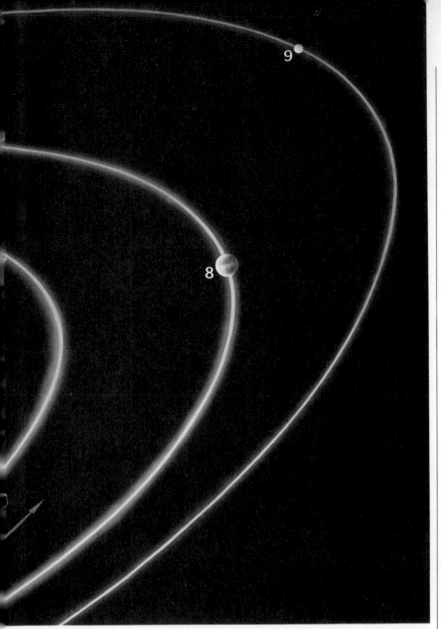

This is an artist's drawing of the planets, in order from the sun.
1. Mercury
2. Venus
3. Earth
4. Mars
5. Jupiter
6. Saturn
7. Uranus
8. Neptune
9. Pluto

sizes. Some of the marbles are circling close to the rim. Others are circling close to the center of the plate. The circling marbles are much like the orbiting planets. However, each planet has its own orbit. And each planet orbits at a different speed. Scientists know where any

3. Which is the hottest planet? Which is the coldest planet?

planet will be at any time. The pull of **gravitational** (grav′ə tā′shə nəl) **attraction** keeps the planets in orbit. This pull is between the sun and each planet.

THE PLANETS IN ORDER

Mercury is the planet nearest the sun. It is also the solar system's hottest and fastest-moving planet. It orbits the sun every 88 days. So Mercury makes four orbits while Earth makes one. In 1974 the spacecraft Mariner 10 took pictures of Mercury. These pictures showed that Mercury looks much like our moon.

This is a picture of Mercury. It was made by putting together 18 smaller pictures. They were taken by the spacecraft Mariner 10 as it flew past Mercury. Can you see where some of the small pictures are?

Venus is between Earth and Mercury. It is sometimes called Earth's sister planet. This is because it is about the same size as Earth. Thick clouds cover Venus. The clouds reflect sunlight. This makes Venus look very bright. Venus is often seen just after sunset. It is then called the evening star. Why is this wrong?

What do the clouds show about Venus? They show that Venus has some kind of **atmosphere** (at´ mə sfir). An atmosphere is a layer of gases surrounding a planet. Space probes show that this atmosphere is very hot. The atmosphere could be as hot as 500°C. Water boils at 100°C.

The third planet from the sun is **Earth.** You could fill many books with what we know about Earth. Life is possible on Earth for many reasons. On Earth, it is neither too hot nor too cold. Plants and animals are found in most places on Earth. Except for Mars, the more distant planets are too cold for life.

Earth also has the right materials to support life. Plants and animals need carbon dioxide, oxygen, and water to live. Earth has plenty of these things.

An astronaut took this picture while standing on the moon. The moon is the bare brown land in the foreground. The half-lit ball in the sky is our home—Earth. The white circular and speckled areas over the earth are clouds. The astronaut took this picture without using a flash. What light did he use to take this picture?

Venus and the moon in the evening sky. Why does Venus look smaller?

This is a real picture of Mars. It was taken by the Viking 1 lander. The lander is still on Mars.

What about **Mars?** Mars is the fourth planet from the sun. The landing of Viking I on Mars has told us much about Mars. Soil samples taken by Viking II show that life as we know it does not exist on Mars. Daytime temperatures in summer may reach nearly 27°C. That is like a hot July day on Earth. But night temperatures, even in summer, may drop to −75°C. That is colder than the North Pole, even in winter.

Jupiter is the largest planet in the solar system. It has bands of color. Notice the Great Red Spot on its surface. No one knows what the spot is.

Saturn is the second-largest planet in the solar system. How is Saturn different from the other planets?

The next four planets are **Jupiter, Saturn, Uranus** (yu̇r′ə nəs), and **Neptune.** They are the **major planets.** Each is hundreds of times larger than Earth.

Pluto was the last planet to be discovered. It is usually the farthest planet from the sun. But its orbit changes. Between 1979 and 1998, Pluto will be closer to the sun than Neptune will be. Pluto is about the same size as Mercury.

4. Which are the four major planets? Why are they called "major" planets?

PLANETS AND ENERGY

You have learned that our sun is a star. You also know that stars are large masses of glowing gases. The stars give off great energy. Some of that energy comes to us as light. But planets do not give off light.

At night, you may see Venus, Mars, Jupiter, or Saturn. The light you see from these planets is reflected sunlight. The moon does not give off light either. It, too, reflects light from the sun.

Some scientists think some large planets may produce heat energy. Jupiter is one of those planets. Its matter may be pressed very tightly together. This may cause heat energy to be given off.

THE SKY'S LITTLE LEAGUE

Are there other members of the solar system besides the sun, the planets, and their moons? Look at the space between Mars and Jupiter on page 14. Scientists have discovered many planetlike objects in this region. They are called **planetoids** (plan′ ə toidz). Most of them are only a few meters or kilometers wide. However, a few are as much as 400 kilometers wide.

Other objects that travel around the sun are **comets** (kom′ itz). Can you imagine a pile of gravel flying through the air? If you can, you have an idea of what a comet is like. Comets are often very large. They have heads and usually very long tails. Some take thousands of years to orbit the sun. Others take much less time. When a comet nears the sun, energy from

the sun strikes the head. The energy pushes some of the lighter matter out of the head. This forms the tail. One famous comet is **Halley's comet.** This comet makes regular trips around the sun. It comes near the earth every 76 years. It is expected again in 1986. How old will you be then? When was it last seen in the sky?

Bennett's comet is one of the brightest discovered in recent years. It seems to take about 1000 years to orbit the sun. How does this compare with the time it takes for Halley's comet to orbit the sun?

5. What are two famous comets?

METEORS AND METEORITES

Sometimes small objects in space come very near the earth. Have you ever seen a flash of light in the night sky? It only lasts a second. Some nights the sky seems filled with these streaks. Many people call them shooting stars. They are really small bits of stony material. When they enter the earth's atmosphere, they are

This iron meteorite could be called a "visitor from outer space." Is it bigger, or smaller, than it was when it entered the atmosphere?

called **meteors** (mē′tē ərs). A meteor gets burning hot as it falls through the atmosphere. Usually, this heat burns up the meteor. Some meteors, however, do reach the surface of the earth. A meteor that hits the earth is called a **meteorite** (mē′tē ə rīt). Large meteorites have left large holes, or **craters** (krā′tərs), when they landed. Most meteorites that land on the earth are tiny. They settle like fine dust all over the earth.

A very large meteorite made this crater. The crater is in Arizona.

HOW FAR IS FAR?

You know that the sun is very large and very far away. But how large is it? How far away is it? To understand distance in space, we must learn about distance on the earth.

In your classroom you probably have a **meterstick** (mē′tər stik). A meterstick is one **meter** (mē′tər) long. Take a meterstick and measure some things. You are taller than one meter. Is your doorway about 1 meter wide? Is your classroom about 3 meters high? How long is your classroom in meters? Suppose you put 1000 metersticks end to end. That would equal 1 **kilometer** (kil′ə mē tər). Short distances on the earth are measured in meters. Long distances are measured in kilometers. Distances between planets are measured in kilometers.

USING YOUR MATH

1. How many centimeters in a meter?
2. How many meters in a kilometer?
3. How many millimeters in a meter?
4. How many millimeters in a centimeter?

TRY THIS

Use a small metric ruler to measure the following objects.
1. The thickness of this book
2. The length of this page
3. The length of this line
4. The size of this bug

Activity 3

How far is a kilometer?

A. You are going to walk 1 kilometer. Your teacher will take you outside. Be sure you wear a coat if it is cool. Stay with your teacher and follow directions.

B. Before you take your walk, answer questions **1** and **2**. Answer the other questions when you come back from your walk.

Answer these before your walk:

1. Your teacher has told you where you will walk. Where do you think the kilometer will end?

2. How long do you think it will take you to walk a kilometer?

Answer these after your walk:

3. Was a kilometer longer or shorter than you thought?

4. The symbol km stands for kilometer. This symbol does not begin with a capital letter. It does not have a period. How far did you walk round trip? Write that distance, using the symbol for kilometer.

HOW BIG IS BIG?

Let's make a model of the earth. Suppose the earth were the size of a tennis ball. Then the sun would be a ball 7 meters across!

Let's think of it another way. Suppose the whole earth was just dry land. There would be no oceans or large rivers. And you could walk all the way around it. Let's say you could walk 12 kilometers every day. How long would it take to walk around it once? About 9 years!

Now suppose the sun was a cool, solid ball. Imagine that you are going to walk

Earth

Walk around once — 9 years

around the sun. Again, you will walk 12 kilometers every day. How long would it take you to walk around the sun once? The answer is 1000 years!

How far away is the sun? Suppose you had a spaceship that could travel 40 000 kilometers in an hour. It would take more than 5 months to reach the sun in this spaceship.

As you can see, the sun is very, very big. It is also very far away. If it were much closer, we would receive too much radiant energy. If it were farther away, we would receive too little energy. But big as it is, the sun is only a medium-sized star.

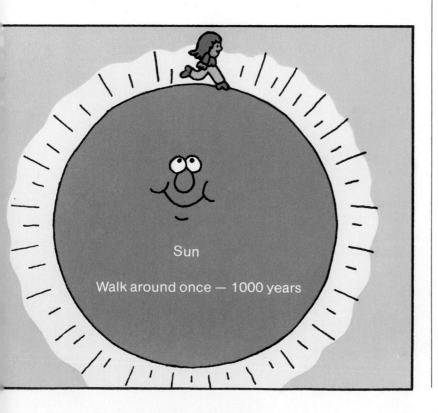

Sun

Walk around once — 1000 years

Movements of the Earth

Each morning you get out of bed. You get dressed. You eat breakfast and come to school. At the end of the school day, you go back home. You move from place to place. But just how does the earth move? You learned in Chapter 1 that planets travel in orbits around the sun.

The earth **revolves** (ri volvs′) around the sun. A complete trip around the sun takes a year. But is this the only way the earth moves? If the sun does not move, what causes night and day?

As the earth moves around the sun, it also spins like a top. This spinning is called **rotation** (rō tā′ shən). All the planets, and even the sun, rotate like tops.

The merry-go-round rotates.
The children revolve.

The top spins or rotates.

The earth, below this spacecraft, revolves around the sun. The spacecraft revolves around the earth. The astronaut revolves around both the earth and the sun.

Activity 4

How can you make a model to show how the planets move?

You need:

Sheet of paper   Crayon or
String   marking pencils
Masking tape

A. Your class will make a model of the solar system. Your teacher will pick 11 students to be the solar system. Nine of you will be planets. One will be the sun, and one the moon.

B. Suppose you are a planet, the sun, or the moon. On a piece of paper, write the name of what you are. Make the letters large. Follow the directions your teacher will give you.

C. All planets will line up in order, from Mercury to Pluto. If you are a planet, be sure you have your name sign. The moon will stay close to Earth. All students who are planets should face the sun.

D. When your teacher tells you, the planets should turn to the right. They should walk slowly in a circle around the sun. All should walk at the same speed. Keep walking until Earth is back where it started. The sun turns around, but does not walk. The moon walks around Earth as Earth moves. When Earth is back where it started, a year has gone by.

Answer these:

1. Which planets did not make a complete circle?

2. Which planets made more than one complete circle?

3. A year is the time it takes to go around the sun once. Each planet's year is different. Which planet has the shortest year? Which has the longest year?

4. How many times did the moon go around the sun? How many times did the moon go around Earth?

Activity 5

How can you show night and day with a globe and a lamp?

You need:
Globe
Lamp, with a 100-watt bulb
Masking tape

Tape

A. Stick a small piece of tape on the globe to show where you live.

B. Hold the globe as shown. The light will be a model for the sun. Have the tape face the light.

C. Stand still. Slowly rotate the globe. Explain to your teacher and classmates why day and night take place.

Answer these:
1. Does the sun have to move in order to have day and night?
2. Why does the sun seem to move across the sky?
3. Is the North Pole at the top of the globe? Where is the South Pole? What does this tell you about the earth?

THE CHANGING SEASONS

Summer, fall, winter, spring. What causes the different seasons? The earth is about the same distance from the sun all year round. Why, then, is it hot in the summer and cold in the winter? To answer this, look at the pictures below.

The two pictures show the sun shining on the same garden. In one, it is twelve o'clock noon on a summer day. In the other, it is noon on a winter day. Which garden gets more radiant energy? Which picture shows summer? Which picture shows winter? In which season would you get a better tan? Now look at a globe. Why is it hot in summer and cold in winter? Try to explain why we have seasons.

6. What is the season when a new year starts?

TIME ZONES

Students in Oregon are eating breakfast. At the same time, students in Maine are eating lunch. Do you know why? Time is different in different places in the United States. Morning comes three hours earlier in Maine than it does in Oregon. Why is this true? It is because people see the sun about three hours earlier in Maine. Look at your globe. See if you can explain why this happens.

As the earth rotates, different parts of the earth receive sunlight. When the sun is nearly overhead, it is twelve o'clock noon. Everyone agrees that morning, noon, and night should have the same "clock time." So time zones were set up for the whole earth. There are 24 time zones. Forty-eight of the United States lie in four of these time zones. The zones are shown in the picture on the next page. What is the difference in time between New York and Chicago? between Denver and Baltimore? between Miami and Los Angeles?

The picture shows the time zones for the United States. Each time zone is a different color. New York, Baltimore, and Miami are in the yellow zone. Chicago is in the orange zone. Denver is in the light-blue zone, Los Angeles is in the dark-blue zone. In which time zone do you live?

TRY THIS
Get a lamp, the globe, and a bit of tape. Put the tape on Maine. Show how Maine could have sunrise while it is still night in California.

7. What time zone do you live in?

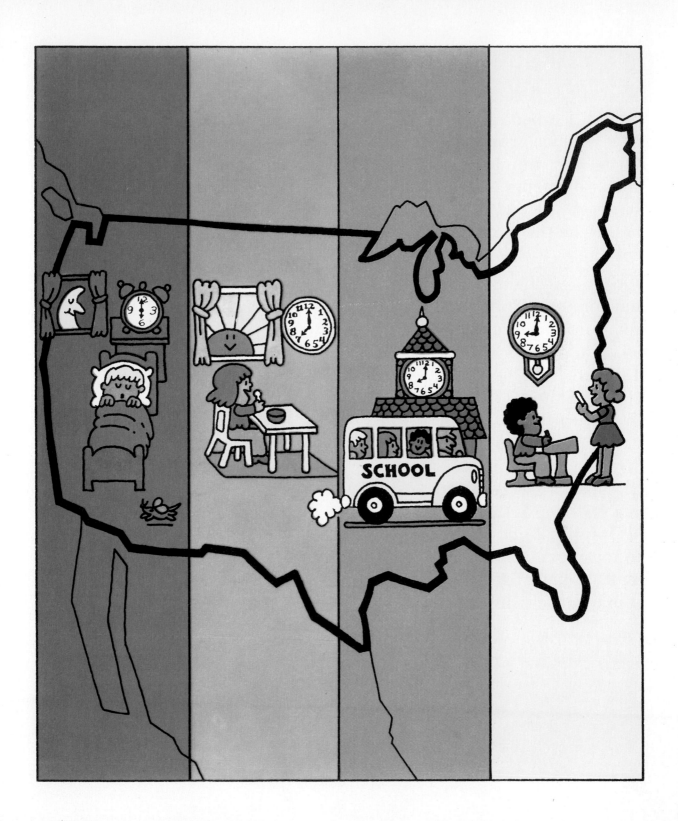

Checking What You Learned

You learned some important new science words in this unit. Write the numbers 1−5 on a sheet of paper. Then read the sentences below. After each number, write the word that correctly completes the sentence. Use these words: comet, crater, gravity, meteor, meteorite, orbit, planet, rotation, time zones.

1. There are 4 _____ in the United States. There are 24 _____ in the world.
2. A _____ could be called a "frozen, flying pile of gravel."
3. The correct name for a shooting star is a _____.
4. It takes 24 hours for the earth to make one _____.
5. If a meteorite hits the earth, it may make a hole called a _____.

CHECKING THE FACTS

Write the numbers 1−5 on a sheet of paper. Then read the sentences below. Decide whether each one is true or false. If it is true, write T next to the number. If it is false, write F.

1. There are nine planets in the solar system.
2. The sun is a star.
3. The sun revolves around the earth.
4. It takes a year for the earth to make one rotation on its axis.
5. The path a planet travels around the sun is called an orbit.

ACTIVITIES TO TRY

1. The astronauts who landed on the moon found many craters there. Some were large. Some were small. You can make some "moon craters." Mix some plaster of Paris until it is about as thick as mud. Pour it into an aluminum-foil pie pan. While the plaster is still wet, drop some stones of different sizes into it. Drop some from just above the plaster. Drop some from far above. When the plaster is dry, take out the stones. Describe the craters you made.

2. Get a bottle, a cork to fit in it, and some stiff wire. Three Styrofoam balls of different sizes will represent the sun, the moon, and the earth. Make a model to show how these three bodies rotate and revolve. The drawing below shows how to set up the model.

IDEAS TO THINK ABOUT

1. The lines that separate the time zones are not always straight. Why? Suppose a time-zone line cut through the middle of a city. What might happen?

2. What is daylight saving time? Find out what it means. Why do we have it?

SCIENCE AND YOU

You are living in the Space Age. Much is known about the universe. But there is still more to learn. Already there are plans for a "space shuttle." You may be a pilot on a space shuttle someday. Or you may be a welder or an electrician who helps build a spacecraft. TV and radio technicians will be needed in the control rooms. Astronomers will be needed to study the bodies in space. Perhaps one day you may work in one of these jobs.

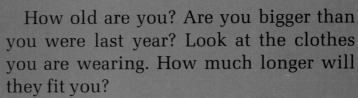

The Changing Earth

How old are you? Are you bigger than you were last year? Look at the clothes you are wearing. How much longer will they fit you?

You are growing every day. You cannot see how much you grow in a short time. But in several years you may be bigger than your parents. You will be much older then. You can see changes in people as they get older.

The earth changes, too, as it gets older. The earth has been changing for many millions of years. Some of these changes you can see. Others you can't see. In what ways is the earth changing? Look at the pictures. How do they show that the earth is changing?

The top picture was taken near a volcano in Iceland. At the far left is a picture of the shore at Cape Cod. The rock at the right is called Mushroom Rock.

1

How the Earth Changes

The only part of the earth you've seen is the outer layer. This outer layer of earth is called the **crust.** The crust is the thin "skin" of rocks that covers all the earth's surface. The crust is as much as 50 kilometers thick in some places. In other places, it is as little as 5 kilometers thick. Have you ever seen rocks in a cliff? The crust is made up of rocks like these.

Look at a globe or map of the world. You can see that most of the crust is covered with water. The ocean bottom is covered with a thin layer of soil. This is true of the land as well. The soil is on top of the rocks. There is broken rock in this soil. Why is crust a good name for the earth's outer layer?

This big rock was once lava in a volcano. The lava cooled and hardened. Later the soft land around it wore away. What could have worn it away?

INSIDE THE EARTH

Underneath the crust is a layer of much heavier rock. This layer is called the **mantle** (man′ təl). The earth's mantle is much thicker than the crust. It is about 3000 kilometers thick. This is about the distance from Washington, D.C., to Salt Lake City, Utah.

Below the mantle is the **core** of the earth. No one knows for sure what the earth's core is like. Most scientists believe it is about 6400 kilometers across. The core is thought to be made mainly of iron. Scientists also believe it is very hot at the center of the earth.

Suppose you went into a mine deep in the earth. You go down one or two kilometers. What kind of clothes would you wear to be comfortable? Would you want a fur coat or a bathing suit? Miners know that it gets hotter as you go into a mine. In fact, some of the deepest mines must be air-conditioned. Why, do you think, does the earth get hotter as you go deeper?

The mantle and the core are far beneath our feet. We are not sure how they change. Yet we see the crust every day. Many things change the earth's crust. If we look carefully, we can see many ways the earth changes.

1. Which layer of the earth is the thickest?

The outer layer of the earth is called the crust. In most places it is many kilometers thick. Suppose the earth were the size of an apple. Then the crust would be only as thick as the apple's skin.

The mantle of the earth is just below the crust. Many scientists think the mantle is partly soft. They also think the crust may be floating on the mantle.

The core of the earth cannot be studied easily. It is beneath 3000 kilometers of rock. Some scientists think the earth's core is liquid metal. Others think the core may be solid.

In the year A.D. 79, the Italian city of Pompeii was destroyed. It was covered by lava from a volcano. How can you tell this happened very quickly?

VOLCANOES

You know it is hot deep inside the earth. The great heat melts some of the rocks. Melted rock deep inside the earth is called **magma** (mag′ mə). The heavy rock around the magma pushes it up. Sometimes it squeezes up through cracks in the earth's crust. It flows out over the land. Then it is called **lava** (lä′ və). When the lava cools, it becomes solid rock. Often mountains are made from the piles of lava that cooled. The mountains are called **volcanoes** (vol kā′ nōs). Sometimes melted rock does not spurt out of the earth. After rising, it cools slowly underground. One kind of melted rock that cools into solid rock underground is called **granite** (gran′ it).

WATER HELPS MAKE ROCKS

You learned how some rocks form from melted rock. Some rocks also form in the sea. Rivers and streams flow to the sea. They carry mud, sand, and pebbles with them. When these materials reach the sea, they settle to the bottom. Ocean bottoms are covered with mud, sand, and pieces of rock. This material is called **sediment** (sed′ ə mənt).

Year after year the sediment piles up. Layers of sediment form on the bottom of the ocean. The sediment becomes many meters thick. Much time goes by. The weight of the top layers presses on the bottom layers. The mud, sand, and pebbles are squeezed tightly together. After a long time, the sediment becomes rock. Rock formed in this way is called **sedimentary** (sed ə men′ tər ē) **rock.**

2. Where do sedimentary rocks form?

Water from a river flows into the ocean. There it slows down. Sediment settles out of the water when this happens.

Sediment

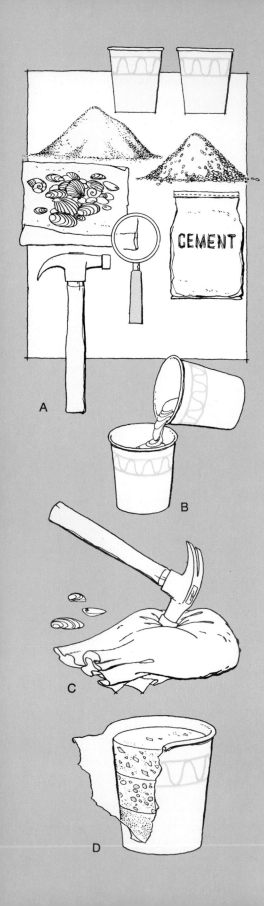

Activity 6

How is sedimentary rock formed?

You need:

2 paper cups	Pebbles
Quick-drying cement	Seashells
Sand	Water
Newspaper	Hand lens
Hammer	Piece of cloth

A. Cover your desk or table with newspaper. Mix a little cement, sand, and water in a paper cup. Pour this into another cup.

B. After the cement sets, mix a little cement, pebbles, and water. Pour this into the second cup as the next layer.

C. Place some shells in a piece of cloth. Break up the shells. Mix the broken shells with a little cement and water. Pour this into the second paper cup as the third layer. Put the cup out of the way overnight.

D. Tear away the cup from the rock you made. Look at the rock with a hand lens. Break up the rock. Look at the pieces with a hand lens.

Answer these:

1. How was your rock like sedimentary rock?

2. How would these bits of matter collect in nature to form rock?

3. How would you describe your rock?

WATER BREAKS UP ROCKS

You have learned that running water can carry sediment. This sediment can be pressed into rocks. But where does the sediment come from? It comes from soil and other rocks.

Water has been breaking up rocks since the first raindrop fell. The breaking up of rocks is called **weathering.** Bits of rock and soil are carried away in many ways. This movement is called **erosion** (i rō′zhən). Rivers and streams can carry tons of soil and broken rocks many kilometers. The Mississippi River moves over 500 million metric tons of material each year.

In spring the snow melts. Often there are also heavy rains. Then the rivers cannot carry this added water. The rivers overflow and flood the land. The flooding washes away even more soil and rocks. As the flooded land dries up, much sediment is left behind.

Ocean waves are moving water. They are always breaking on the seacoast. Some shore areas have no sand at all. In other places, waves have washed sand and rocks onto the shore.

Water has greatly changed the face of the earth in the past. It will keep doing so in the years ahead.

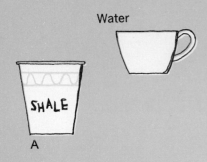

A

B

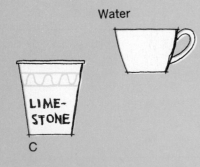

C

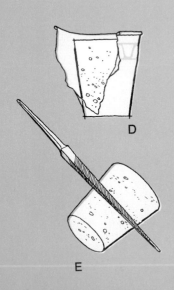

D

E

Activity 7

What kind of sedimentary rock wears away the easiest?

You need:

3 paper cups	Water
Cement	Triangular file
Sand	Graduated cylinder
Lime	

A. You are going to make 3 kinds of "sedimentary rock." Then you will see which wears away the easiest.

B. Mix 50 mL of cement with 150 mL of water. Pour this into one paper cup. Call this rock "shale."

C. Mix 25 mL of cement with 75 mL of sand. Add 150 mL of water. Pour this into another cup. Call this "sandstone."

D. Add 150 mL of water to 25 mL of cement. Then mix in 75 mL of lime. Pour this into the third cup. Call this "limestone."

E. Let the cups stand overnight. Tear away the paper cups from the rocks.

F. Rub each rock 10 times with a triangular file. Pull the file in the same direction each time. The file acts like water wearing away the rocks.

Answer these:

1. Tell what each rock looked like.
2. Which rock was worn away the easiest?
3. How would water act on these rocks?

These rocks look like icicles. But of course they are not. They formed in caves. These caves are the Carlsbad Caverns in New Mexico.

GROUNDWATER AND ROCKS

You can see water running in rivers and streams. Some water is deep down in the earth's crust. This water is called **groundwater.** It cannot easily be seen. Sometimes people drill holes down into the ground to make wells. If they reach groundwater, they pump it up.

Groundwater has many minerals in it. The water can seep through the roofs of caves. Some of the water evaporates. The minerals are left behind. They form stones that look like icicles. Some of these point down from the roof of the cave. Some of the water drips from these "icicles." It forms stones on the floor of the cave. These stones point up to the roof of the cave.

WIND CHANGES THE EARTH

Have you ever watched a person sandblasting a stone building? Sandblasting cleans the building. A strong blast of air blows sand against the stone. Each grain of sand wears away some dirt from the building.

Sand carried by strong winds can wear away huge rocks. The moving grains of sand grind away bits of rock. This may take thousands of years. But one day the rock will be worn away.

Sand can be carried great distances by wind. Grains of sand may travel hundreds of kilometers. Dust is blown even farther than sand. Why, do you think, is this so? Dust in the air may be carried across whole continents. Wind moves great amounts of sand and dust. Wind can pile sand into **dunes** (dünz) hundreds of meters thick.

Activity 8

How can wind move sand?

You need:

2 pie pans	2 large cardboard boxes
Flour	2 battery-powered fans
Fine sand	

A

A. Put flour in one pie pan. Make it about 2 cm deep. Put the same amount of sand in the other pan. Put the pans on a table near the edge. The pans should be about a meter apart. Stand a cardboard box about a meter behind each pan. Make sure the inside of each box faces a pan.

B. Pick up a fan. Stand about 8 meters from the table. Face one of the pans. Your fan should be held level with the pan.

C. Turn on your fan. Slowly walk toward the table. Stop when the flour or sand starts moving. Notice which moves first.

D. Move a little closer to the table. Notice what happens in each pan.

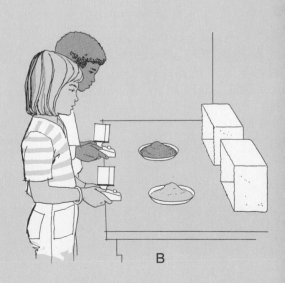

B

Answer these:

1. Which moved first—the flour or the sand?
2. How did the flour and sand blow?

51

ICE CHANGES THE EARTH

In many places on the earth it is very cold in winter. Snow falls and is packed into ice. The ice builds up and becomes very thick. A **glacier** (glā′ shər) is formed. Some glaciers cover large areas of land. They cover the rocks and soil on the earth's surface. Glaciers may cover whole valleys. Long ago, large glaciers covered parts of the United States. Some of these glaciers were 2 kilometers thick.

Some glaciers get larger. Others melt and get smaller. How can you tell that the one below is getting smaller?

A glacier could be called a "river of ice." This Swiss glacier flows into a lake.

Mountain glaciers slide slowly downhill. Other glaciers slide across the earth's surface. They move too slowly to be noticed. As glaciers move, they drag along the rocks and soil beneath them. Heavy glaciers scratch and dig at the earth's surface. Streams and rivers start from melting glaciers. The streams carry away the rocks and soil in them. Often large lakes are left when glaciers melt. The Great Lakes formed long ago from the movement of glaciers. Find the Great Lakes on your class map.

TRY THIS

Sprinkle some sand into an ice-cube tray. Fill the tray with water. Put the tray in the freezer. After the cubes are frozen, take them out of the tray. Rub the bottom of the cubes on a plasterboard. How can this be compared to the movement of a glacier?

2

Rocks and Soil

Many kinds of rocks make up the earth's crust. Almost everywhere you look, you see rocks. There are brightly colored rocks. There are dull, gray rocks. Some rocks are hard. Some are soft enough to be scratched by your fingernail. Some rocks are rough like sand or like broken glass. Other rocks are smooth like the top of your desk. There are big rocks and little rocks. Big rocks are called **boulders** (bōl′dərs). Some boulders are bigger than your classroom.

Soil is also an important part of the earth's crust. Soil is formed as rocks are broken up. You know there are many different-colored rocks. Does this help you understand why soils have different colors too?

The big rocks along this river were once part of these mountains. How did they get here? What else has been moved in the picture?

Activity 9

How are rocks different from each other?

You need:
3 rocks (brought from home)
Nail
Hand lens
Vinegar, in a dropper bottle

A. Find a classmate to be your partner. Together you will use 6 rocks in this activity.

B. See how many rocks you can scratch with a nail. See if the rocks can scratch the nail. Rocks that can scratch the nail probably contain **quartz** (kwôrts). Quartz is a glassy mineral found in many rocks.

C. Take the rocks that you can scratch. Put some vinegar in the scratches. Look at each scratch with your hand lens. See if the rock fizzes or bubbles. If it does, it probably contains **calcite** (kal′ sīt). Calcite is a mineral found in limestone and other rocks.

Answer these:
1. How many rocks were harder than the nail? How many were softer?
2. Did any of the rocks contain calcite? How could you tell?

56

DIFFERENT KINDS OF ROCKS

In the last chapter you learned about volcanoes. The lava from volcanoes was once melted rock material. Granite was formed underground. It was once melted rock material, too. Rocks formed from melted rock material are called **igneous** (ig′ nē əs) **rocks.** Lava and granite are two kinds of igneous rocks.

There are other kinds of rocks. You learned that rocks can be broken down by water, wind, and ice. The rocks are broken into sediments. These sediments get pressed together to form rocks. This kind of rock is called sedimentary rock.

Sandstone is a sedimentary rock. It forms from sand that came from older, broken rocks. Look closely at a piece of sandstone. It looks grainy. The grains are cemented together. If you scratch a piece of sandstone, you get sand. Take the sandstone and rub the nail. It will scratch the nail. Sandstone is made up mostly of quartz. And quartz is harder than the nail.

Limestone is another sedimentary rock. It often forms from the bones and shells of sea animals. Put vinegar on a piece of limestone. It will bubble or fizz. That's because there is calcite in limestone. It reacts with vinegar to form bubbles of gas. This gas is **carbon dioxide.**

3. What are rocks formed from melted material called?

The rock above is a piece of natural quartzite. It was once sandstone. The rock below is polished marble. It was once limestone. How are these two rocks alike? How are they different?

This is a fossil. What animal formed this fossil?

Sometimes the bodies of sea animals do not break up. They settle to the bottom as they were in life. They mix in with sediment that will become rock. Such shells and bones are called **fossils** (fos′ əls). The fossils are not greatly changed when the sediment becomes rock. Finding a rock that has fossils in it is like finding a history book. We can study the fossils. We can learn about animals and plants that lived long ago.

Sandstone and limestone are often found far inland. Many mountains are made of sandstone, limestone, or other sedimentary rocks. But sedimentary rocks formed in the sea. How can they be found in mountains? Sometimes the crust of the earth is pushed up. Forces far beneath the crust can do this. The ocean bottom is lifted far above the water. The sedimentary rock becomes part of the land.

Sometimes igneous and sedimentary rocks are buried deep in the earth. Heat and pressure from overlying rocks change the igneous and sedimentary rocks. They become new rocks. These new rocks are called **metamorphic** (met ə môr′ fik) **rocks.** Some metamorphic rocks are quartzite, marble, and slate.

Gneiss (nīs) is a metamorphic rock. It was once granite. What helped change it to gneiss?

HOW SOIL IS MADE

Most of the rocks in the earth's crust are covered with soil. In some places, the soil is hundreds of meters thick. In others, it is only a few centimeters deep. Where do you think soil comes from?

Most large plants grow in soil. Most animals use plants for food. Without soil, we would not have very much food.

Look at a handful of soil. Run it through your fingers. How does it feel? Look at the soil under a hand lens. What does it look like?

Soil is made from bits of rock mixed with plant and animal matter. This matter has decayed. Minerals are put back into the soil when something decays. There are also many small living plants and animals in the soil. These are really part of the soil.

Soil forms very slowly. Wind, water, and temperature changes help make soil. Look at the rocks around you. Millions of years from now, they may be soil.

MANY KINDS OF SOIL

Soil is not the same everywhere. You may have seen different kinds of soil. **Sand, clay,** and **loam** are different kinds

4. What is soil made of?

of soil. Soil near the top of the ground is different from deep soil. The layer on top is usually best for growing things. It is called **topsoil.**

Sand does not hold water very well. Have you ever played with sand and water? You know how fast water runs through sand.

Clay is made up of certain kinds of rock dust. The bits of clay are packed tightly together. Clay can hold much water. When it dries, it cracks. Plants do not grow well in clay.

5. What is loam?

Loam is a mixture of sand, clay, and **humus** (hyü′ məs). Humus is formed from decayed plants and animals. Loam has the water and minerals needed for plant growth.

You will learn more about soil in the next three activities.

This is a compost (kom′ pōst) pile. It contains dead plant and animal material. Why do gardeners make compost piles?

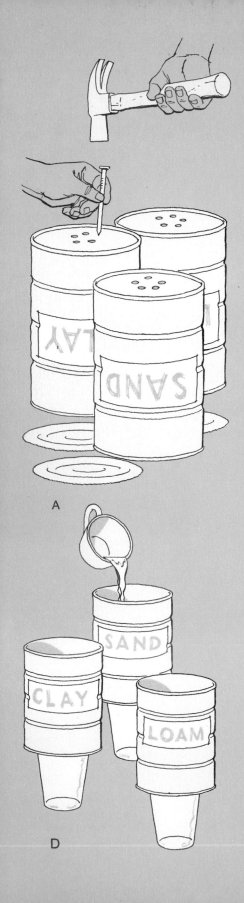

Activity 10

Which kind of soil holds the most water?

You need:

3 large juice cans (all the same size)	Water
	Large nail
Clay	Cup
Sand	Clock or watch
Loam	Paper towels
3 plastic tumblers	Hammer

A. Punch nail holes in the bottoms of the 3 juice cans.

B. Fill one can with clay, one with sand, and one with loam.

C. Place each can on a tumbler. Make sure the holes are over the mouth of the tumbler.

D. Slowly pour 1 cup of water into each can. Wait for 1 hour.

E. Record what you see in the tumblers. Pour the soil onto paper towels. Feel each soil sample.

Answer these:

1. Which tumbler had the most water?
2. Which kind of soil held the most water?
3. How did each kind of soil feel?
4. Which kind of soil would be best for growing plants?

Activity 11

How can you measure how tightly soil is packed together?

You need:

Some Tinkertoys
Wide rubber band
Wooden dowel
Sandpaper

Scissors
Meterstick
Different soil
    samples

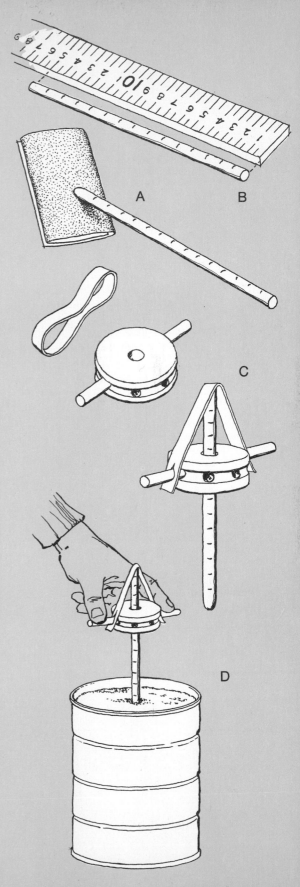

A. You are going to make a soil tester. It will measure how tightly packed soil is. Get a wooden dowel about 15 cm long. Sand one end of the dowel so that it is rounded.

B. Put the meterstick alongside the dowel, as shown. Make a mark for every centimeter on the dowel.

C. Take a Tinkertoy spool, two short Tinkertoy sticks, and the rubber band. Cut the rubber band. Put these together as shown.

D. Push your soil tester down into one soil sample. Make sure the dowel moves easily through the hole in the spool. Count the number of marks the spool moves before the stick goes into the soil.

E. Repeat step **D**. Use other kinds of soil.

Answer these:

1. How many marks did the spool move for each soil sample?

2. List the soils according to how they are packed together. Place the most tightly packed one first.

Activity 12

How can soil be made to grow plants better?

You need:

6 flowerpots	Metric ruler
12 bean seeds	Sand
Fertilizer	Loam
Clay	Poster board
Graduated cylinder	Crayon or felt-tip pen

A. Mark off 1-cm spaces around the edges of the poster board. Draw lines from each of the points. This will be your scale.

B. Fill 2 flowerpots with clay. Fill 2 more with sand. Fill the last 2 with loam. Add 2 mL of dry fertilizer to one pot in each pair. Mix the fertilizer and soil in the pots. Number the pots. Put an X on each pot that has fertilizer.

C. Plant 2 bean seeds in each pot. Be sure to plant them all at the same depth. Put the pots in the sun. Water them daily.

D. When the seeds start growing, put the scale behind each pot. Color in the squares to show each plant's height.

Answer these:

1. In which pot did the seeds grow first?
2. In which pot did the seeds grow best?
3. How did the seeds with fertilizer in each pair grow? What was the difference?
4. How much did each plant grow?

This is Bryce Canyon in Utah. It was formed by weathering and erosion. What caused the weathering and erosion?

SOIL AND EROSION

You have learned that rocks can be broken up to form soil. Movement of the soil is one kind of erosion. This kind of erosion is usually helpful. It provides the soil that plants need. Some erosion is harmful. Sometimes water washes away good topsoil. Only clay, sandy soil, or bare rock is left. Plants grow poorly when the topsoil is gone.

Several things can cause harmful erosion. Forest fires and bad logging are two examples. They both take away the plants that hold the soil. With good logging, seedlings replace the trees that were cut. When farmers plow their land, erosion can take place. Farmers can help stop the washing away of good topsoil. They can plow across hills instead of up and down. This is called **contour** (kon′ tùr) **plowing.** How could contour plowing help stop harmful erosion?

TRY THIS

Get a tray filled with bare soil. Get another tray with grass growing in it. Do plants really stop erosion? Try to explain your answer.

65

Checking What You Learned

You learned some new science words in this unit. Some of them are listed in column B below. Write the numbers 1 – 5 on a sheet of paper. Read the phrases listed in column A. Decide which word in column B best matches each phrase in column A. Write the correct word next to each number on your paper. (You need not use all the words listed in column B.)

A	B
1. A river of ice	humus
2. Decayed plant and animal material	magma
3. The print of a once-living plant or animal	limestone
4. Melted rock inside a volcano	glacier
5. Rocks changed by heat and pressure	metamorphic
	fossil
	sedimentary
	erosion

Write the numbers 1 – 5 on a sheet of paper. Then read each of the sentences below. After each number, write the word that correctly completes the sentence.

1. Rocks that form from sand being cemented together under water are called _____.
2. The rich, black dirt in which plants grow is called _____.
3. The center of the earth is the _____.
4. The movement of rock and soil from one place to another is called _____.
5. The melted rock that flows from a volcano and hardens as it cools is _____.

ACTIVITIES TO TRY

1. Collect some samples of soil from different places in your town. Get some from your backyard. Get some from your school playground. Try to get some from a farm and from an empty lot. Look at the samples with a magnifying glass. Rub some of each sample between your fingers. Also smell each sample. Tell how the samples are alike. Tell how they are different.

2. Begin a rock collection. Get as many different kinds of rocks as you can. Then go to the library. Find a book that will help you learn the names of your rocks. Label each rock. Put your rocks in an egg carton or a large, flat box. Keep adding to your collection when you go on trips.

IDEAS TO THINK ABOUT

1. Fossils show what life was like many years ago. Find Kansas and Nebraska on a map of the United States. Many fossils of large ocean animals are found in those states. What does this tell you about that area? How has the land there changed?

2. Good topsoil contains decayed plants and animals. Why do farmers sometimes plow under old cornstalks and other plants? Learn some other ways that humus is added to the topsoil.

SCIENCE AND YOU

Are you interested in the way the earth changes? There are many interesting jobs in earth science. Geologists study rocks and soil. Paleontologists study fossils to learn about the past life on the earth. Today you hear a lot about seismologists. They study earthquakes. People who take care of the land are important, too. County agricultural agents and soil scientists do this.

Plants

Plants and animals are living things. But why are they called "living"? One reason is that they grow. Do you know what the biggest living things are? They are the redwood trees in California. Some of these trees are more than 76 meters tall. This is taller than fifty people standing on each other's shoulders. It is about twenty-five times higher than your classroom. Redwood trees are bigger than any animal on the earth.

But how small are the smallest plants? Most small plants live in water. They live in oceans, rivers, lakes, and ponds. Hundreds of these plants may live in a drop of water.

These giant redwoods are some of the oldest living things on the earth. This picture was taken at Humboldt Redwood State Park in California.

Plants and the Environment

This picture was taken as an airplane flew over an orchard. You can see many different things in this picture. However, nearly all of them have something in common. Can you tell what it is? Nearly everything you can see in this picture is a plant! What is the one big thing that is not made from a plant? Name the plants you can see. Name the things that come from plants.

Nearly everywhere you go, you will find plants. They are in parks, gardens, and yards. They grow wild in fields and along roads. Some tiny plants float in the air. Other plants grow in the cracks in sidewalks. Some even grow on rocks. You may have some plants growing in your home. Someone must take care of indoor plants.

An apple orchard in New York State. What kinds of care do these plants get?

Some bananas grow wild. Bananas grow in the very hot and wet regions of the world. It must be hot all year round.

PLACES TO LIVE

Where could you find a cactus plant? Where do ferns grow wild? Should corn be planted in bright sunlight or in shade? Why won't bananas grow in Canada?

All green plants need the same things to live. They must have water, air, light, and warmth. Look at the pictures. Do you think all these plants have the same amount of water? Which plants get the most sunlight? Which plants grow in the warmest place?

Plant roots, stems, and leaves hold much water. You can squeeze liquid out of many plants. The liquid is mostly water. Green plants use water to make food. Water is also used to carry the food inside the plants.

This is a cornfield in the Midwest. Corn also needs much moisture. And it should be hot when the corn grows. But it does not have to be hot all year round.

The cacti above and the ferns below grow in different places. How are the places in which they grow different?

Few plants grow where water is always frozen. Plants cannot use frozen water. Ice cannot move in plants. So plants need a warm place to grow. Some plants grow best where it is cool. What plants grow best in cool places? What plants grow best in warm places? Why do orchids and bananas grow in the same kind of place?

Most farm crops grow in bright sunlight. They do not grow well in shade. Coffee bushes grow best in shade. So they are often grown in the shade of trees. Corn does not grow well in the shade. Do you think coffee bushes would grow well in a cornfield? Would coffee or corn grow better in your classroom?

All plants need some room to grow. Yet some plants can grow in a small space.

ROOM TO GROW

Plants grow close together in some places. They grow far apart in other places. There can be many reasons for these differences. You can investigate some of the reasons. Some reasons are more important than others.

Many green plants start growing from seeds. Nearly always, one plant grows from one seed. So, many seeds are needed if many plants are to grow. If a few seeds are planted, only a few plants will grow. Suppose you see a field with only a few plants. What does this tell you about the number of seeds that were planted?

Most green plants make many seeds. A maple tree makes thousands of seeds each year. Most of the seeds fall near the tree. Only a few will grow to be trees. The same is true of dandelions. Each dandelion flower makes hundreds of seeds. Suppose all dandelion seeds grew. The earth would be covered with dandelions. But you know this does not happen. Not all dandelion seeds become plants.

In the desert, plants grow far apart. But if you picked up some desert soil, you would find many seeds in it. Most of those seeds never begin to grow. Only a few plants would live if the seeds did grow. Why, do you think, do few seeds grow into plants in the desert?

Activity 13

Which plants grow best?

You need:

3 small flowerpots   3 saucers
Tomato seeds   Houseplant fertilizer
Vermiculite   Marking pen

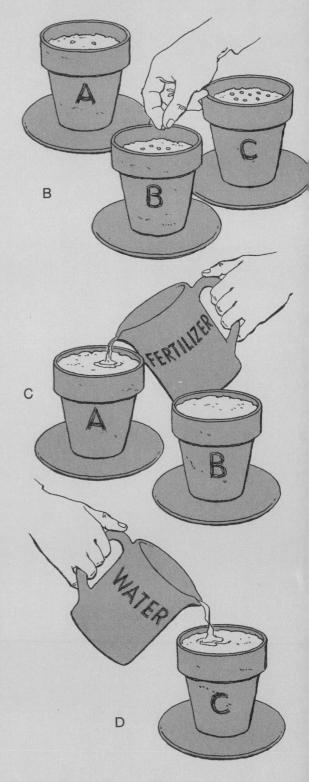

A. Nearly fill the flowerpots with vermiculite. Vermiculite is made from a rock.

B. Mark each pot A, B, or C. Put 2 seeds in pot A. Put 8 seeds in pots B and C. Cover the seeds with a thin layer of vermiculite.

C. Pour fertilizer water on pots A and B. Your teacher will mix the fertilizer and water for you.

D. Water pot C with plain water. Do not water the plants too much. The saucers should be dry most of the time.

E. Put the pots together in a sunny place. Wait 3 weeks before you answer the questions below.

Answer these:

1. In which pot do the plants have the thickest stems? In which pot do the plants have the darkest color?

2. In which pot could a plant get the most water and fertilizer?

3. Pots B and C should have about the same number of plants. Are the plants in one pot more healthy than those in the other pot? How can you tell?

4. Why are some plants more healthy?

HELPING PLANTS GROW

Farmers grow many plants close together. But sometimes the soil doesn't
have enough minerals. Then farmers put
fertilizer on their fields. Fertilizer has the
minerals plants need to grow. By adding
minerals, more plants can grow in a small
space.

Farmers grow more plants in a small
space in another way. Many plants need
much water. They may need more water
than falls as rain. Extra water can be
added by **irrigation** (ir ə gā′ shən). With
fertilizer, irrigation, and sunlight, many
plants can grow in a small place.

Plants may die if there is not enough
fertilizer, water, and sunlight. But
too much water and fertilizer is equally
bad. Then plants do not grow well either.
Healthy plants have the right amounts
of what they need to live.

Do you know someone who raises
plants? This person may have many
plants in the house or garden. Someone else may have trouble growing
plants. What makes this difference? Their
plants and seeds may come from the
same store. They may use the same fertilizers. Both may give their plants enough
water.

People who raise many plants usually know much about them. They know what plants need. They know the kinds of soil in which plants grow best. They know how much water they need. They know whether their plants need sunlight or shade. They also know what temperatures are best for plants. They give their plants all the things that help them grow well.

In many areas, plants do not get enough water from rain. Extra water can be given by irrigation. These young wheat plants are being irrigated.

SPECIAL PLANTS

No two places on the earth are exactly alike. Some places have little water. Other places have much water. Some places are hot. Other places are cool. In some places the soil is deep. In other places there is only a thin layer of soil.

There is some kind of plant almost everywhere on the earth. But different plants grow in different places.

The roots of these plants are very long. Why do they grow deep under the sand?

This is a prairie in Kansas. How is this grass like the grain in the picture on page 79? How is it different?

Plants that need little water can grow in dry places. They die if the soil is too wet. Some desert plants store water. Other desert plants have very long roots. These roots reach the water deep in the soil. Some desert plants live only a few weeks. Their seeds start growing after a rain. They grow flowers in a few days. The seeds from the flowers stay alive for many years. They do not grow until there is more rain.

Much of the land on the earth is flat. Hot, dry winds blow over these flatlands in summer. In winter, the winds are cold and dry. Most of the plants in these places are grass. The stems of most grass plants are under the ground. Soil protects the stems during cold, dry winters. The leaves above the ground bend with the wind. How does this protect the plants? Why do few trees grow here?

A forest is very different from flat, dry land. Leaves of trees shade the ground. The ground under the trees is called the forest floor. The forest floor holds water and minerals. However, it receives very little sunlight. Some small plants and vines may grow on the forest floor. The vines wind around the trees. They grow upward where there is light. Old vines may grow to the tops of trees. The small plants and vines grow only where the things they need are found.

The young wheat in this field in Texas has not yet ripened. What is the climate like here?

Green Plants— The Food Makers

The picture on the facing page shows a place with many plants. Suppose you could paint a picture like this. What would be the most important color for your picture? You're right. Most of the plants in your picture would be green.

The green plants are an important part of your life. You use parts of many green plants for food. Spinach, cabbage, and lettuce are green leaves you eat. The asparagus and potatoes you eat are stems. Radishes, carrots, and beets are roots. Tomatoes, apples, cucumbers, and peaches are fruits. Corn, dry beans, and peanuts are seeds of green plants. What other leaves, stems, roots, fruits, and seeds do you eat?

These beans are now ready to eat. What care did the girl give the plants as they grew?

You may have some of these plants at home. Can you see the fern and ivy? These plants are growing in a greenhouse. How does a greenhouse protect plants?

Bakery goods are also made from plants. Bread, cookies, cakes, and pies are made with flour. Most flour is made from wheat. Wheat is the seed of a kind of grass. Cereals are made from the seeds of different kinds of grass.

Most people eat some foods that are not parts of plants. Meat, milk, and eggs are not plant parts. Where do meat, milk, and eggs come from? Cows, pigs, sheep, goats, and chickens may be used for meat. Milk may come from cows or goats. Eggs are laid by chickens.

Cows, sheep, and goats eat green plants. Pigs and chickens are fed mostly grain. The seeds of different grasses are called **grain.** Without green plants we would not have meat, milk, or eggs.

These foods are all made from plant materials. What foods do you see here? What plants were used to make these foods?

Activity 14

How can you find starch?

You need:

Test papers, A and B	Cornstarch
Pieces of wood,	Paper towels
plastic, metal,	Iodine solution
and writing paper	Medicine dropper

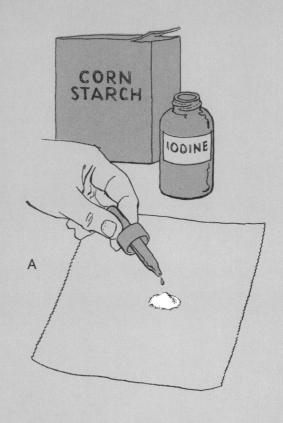

A. Put a paper towel on your desk or table top. Put a pinch of cornstarch on the paper towel. Use the dropper to drop iodine on the starch. Look for a change in color.

B. Your teacher has prepared strips of test paper. There are two kinds. One is called paper A and the other paper B. Paper A is shorter than paper B. One of the strips has been rubbed with starch.

Put the strips of paper on a clear paper towel. Put one drop of iodine on each strip of paper. Find out which strip of paper has starch on it.

C. Use iodine to test wood, plastic, metal, and writing paper. Find out if there is starch in any of these things.

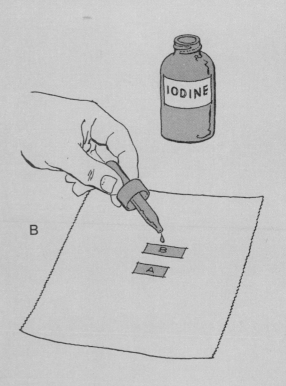

Answer these:

1. What happens when iodine touches starch?

2. Which strip of paper had been rubbed with starch?

3. Was there starch in wood? in metal? in plastic? in writing paper?

THE FOOD OF PLANTS

Starch is in much of the food that you eat. It is made by green plants. Green plants also use starch for food. Where is starch made in a green plant?

Look at the picture at the top. It shows a leaf of a **coleus** (kō′ lē əs) plant. Parts of the leaf are green. Other parts are not.

Look at the middle picture. This is a picture of the same leaf. Much of the color was taken out with alcohol. Most of the green color is now in the beaker.

The bottom picture shows the leaf covered with iodine solution. Starch in the leaf has turned blue-black to brownish-black. Only the green parts of the leaf had starch. How can you tell from the picture?

A chemical gives leaves their green color. This green chemical traps sunlight. Sunlight is one kind of energy. Green plants use this energy to make starch. Starch is food for the plant that makes it. Plants need energy to live and grow. The starch you eat comes from green plants. How does your body use this starch?

These pictures show a coleus leaf. Food is not made in all parts of this leaf. Food is only made where the leaf is green. In the middle picture the whole leaf is the same color. The leaf was soaked in alcohol. This removed much of the chlorophyll. The beaker now holds the dissolved chlorophyll. In the bottom picture the iodine solution shows where the starch is.

Activity 15

Is light needed to make starch?

You need:

Potted plant	Paper clip
Iodine solution	Scissors
Shallow dish	Plastic cup
Piece of black paper	Paper towel
Denatured alcohol	Medicine dropper

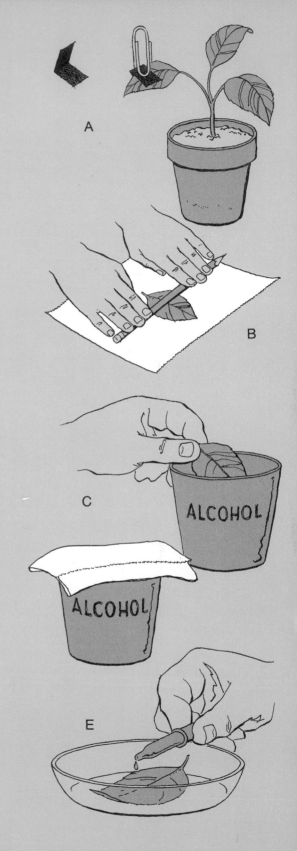

A. Cut a piece of black paper about 1 cm by 3 cm. Fold it in the middle. Put the paper over the edge of a leaf. Clip the paper to the leaf. Put the plant in the sun.

B. Put a paper towel on your desk. Remove the leaf with the paper from the plant. Put the leaf on the towel. Roll a pencil or pen over the leaf a few times.

C. Put the leaf in a cup. Pour alcohol in the cup. Let the leaf soak until tomorrow.

D. Remove the leaf from the alcohol. Look at the color of the alcohol. What color is it?

E. Carefully put the leaf in a dish. Spread a few drops of iodine solution over the leaf. Cover the whole leaf.

Answer these:

1. Why, do you think, did some parts of the leaf make starch?

2. Why, do you think, did the leaf need sunlight to make starch?

3. Make a drawing of your leaf. Show where you found starch.

The young corn plant in the upper picture gets food from the seed. Where does the plant in the lower picture get its food?

Starch in leaves is changed to sugar. The sugar becomes part of the liquid in the plant. This liquid in plants is sometimes called **sap.** Sap can move to all parts of plants. The sugar can be carried to all parts. Sugar can also change back to starch. This happens in different parts of different plants. Starch may be stored in the stems of some plants. It is stored in the roots of others. The seeds of all green plants have stored starch.

GROWING NEW PLANTS

Suppose you are planning a garden. You want to grow vegetables. You will have beans, peas, carrots, and corn. What will you plant to get these plants to grow? You're right if you said seeds. Most green plants start growing from seeds. You might want tomatoes, peppers, or cabbage in your garden. Some people buy small plants of these vegetables. The small plants are planted in the garden. Someone else grew the small plants from seeds.

Most vegetables are grown from seeds. Many flowers are grown from seeds. Seeds are planted to grow grass in lawns. Farmers plant seeds for most of their crops. Almost all weeds grow from seeds. The giant trees of forests started from seeds.

Activity 16

What is in a seed?

You need:

Cut bean seed
Cut corn seed
Hand lens

Iodine solution
Shallow dish
Medicine dropper

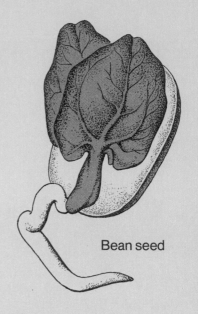

Bean seed

A. Plants that grow from seeds have three main parts. The parts are roots, stems, and leaves. Every seed has a small plant in it. The drawings show the young plants in corn and bean seeds. Look at the young plants in your cut seeds. The hand lens will help you see their parts. Find all the parts shown in the drawings.

B. Seeds have stored food. The stored food is used by the young plants. They need energy when they start to grow. You know how to test for starch. Find out where starch is stored in these seeds.

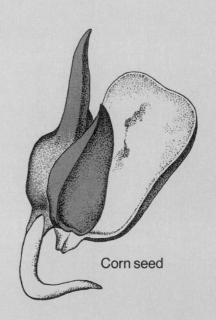

Corn seed

Answer these:

1. Which young plant had leaves most like an old plant?

2. Where did you find stored starch in the seeds? Use drawings of the seeds to show your answer.

3

Nongreen Plants — The Food Users

Most plants you see are green. But there are many plants of other colors. These plants cannot trap energy from light. They cannot make their own food. They are like animals in this way. They get their food from other plants or from animals.

Study the picture on the facing page. It shows some of the more common nongreen plants. Where do you usually find these kinds of plants growing?

A few nongreen plants grow from seeds. They may have roots, stems, and flowers. But few have real leaves. Indian pipes and dodder are plants of this kind.

Indian pipes grow in moist woodlands. In the woods, many trees fall down and die. The wood of these trees rots. Indian pipes use the rotting trees for food.

Mushrooms are nongreen plants. Where do they get their food?

This is a dodder plant. It is a non-green plant that grows on green plants.

A dodder plant may start growing from a seed. The young plant grows until it touches a green plant. Then the dodder grows along the stem of the green plant. Parts of the dodder grow into the green plant. The part of the dodder in the soil dies. Then the dodder takes food from the green plant.

MUSHROOMS AND MOLDS

Mushrooms and molds are nongreen plants. They are called **fungi** (fun′ jī). Fungi do not have roots, stems, leaves, or flowers.

Most fungi get their energy from dead plants. A few kinds get energy from living things. Some mushrooms are good to eat. Others contain poison. They can cause sickness and death. You should not pick mushrooms to eat. Only a trained person should pick mushrooms to eat.

Molds can grow on almost all food. Some molds spoil food. You may have seen molds on bread or fruit. Other molds are used to make food. Blue cheese gets its flavor from a mold. Another mold helps humans fight disease. **Penicillin** (pen ə sil′ in) comes from a mold, shown below.

The fly mushroom (top) is poisonous. The Caesar's mushroom (bottom) is edible.

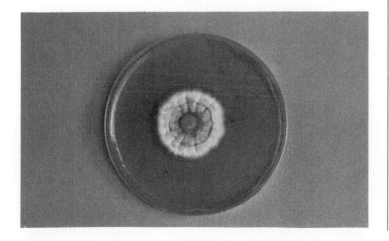

The mold at the left makes a useful medicine that kills germs.

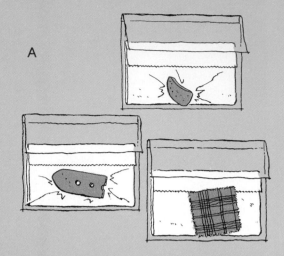

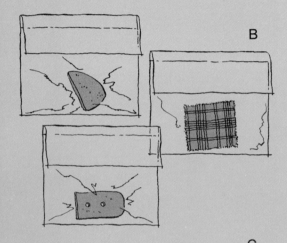

Activity 17

What do fungi need to grow?

You need:

6 plastic sandwich bags	Newspaper
2 lemon or orange peels	Paper towels
2 pieces of leather	Hand lens
2 pieces of woolen cloth	Thumbtacks

A. Put a wet paper towel in each of 3 sandwich bags. Put a peel in the first. Put a piece of leather in the second. Put a piece of woolen cloth in the third.

B. Put a piece of peel in the fourth bag. Put a piece of leather in the fifth bag. Put a piece of woolen cloth in the last bag. There should be no towels in the last 3 bags.

C. Tack the bags to the bulletin board. Put them close together. Cover the bags with several sheets of newspaper.

D. After 5 days, uncover the bags. Do not open them. Use a hand lens to look at the materials in the bags.

Answer these:

1. In which bags did something grow on the materials?

2. What do the fungi look like?

3. In which bags is there no change?

4. What do you think fungi need to grow?

5. Why were the bags covered with newspaper?

Activity 18

How does sunlight affect the growth of fungi?

You need:

2 plastic sandwich bags   Newspaper
2 lemon or orange peels   Rubber bands
Paper towels

A. In the last activity you were asked why the bags were covered. In this activity you will check your answer. Put a wet paper towel and a peel in each bag.

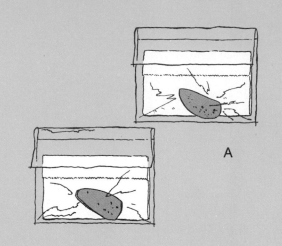

A

B. Wrap one bag in newspaper. Fold all edges to keep light from the bag. Use rubber bands to hold the newspaper.

C. Put the two bags in a sunny place. After 5 days, compare what has happened in the bags.

B

Answer these:

1. Describe what you see in each bag.

2. What must bright light do to mold plants?

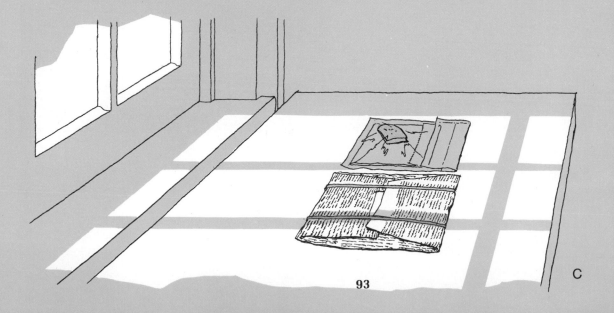

C

93

FUNGI IN YOUR HOME

Fungi do not grow from seeds. They grow from **spores** (spôrz). Spores do not have small plants in them, as do seeds. Millions of spores may come from one plant. Spores are very tiny. They are

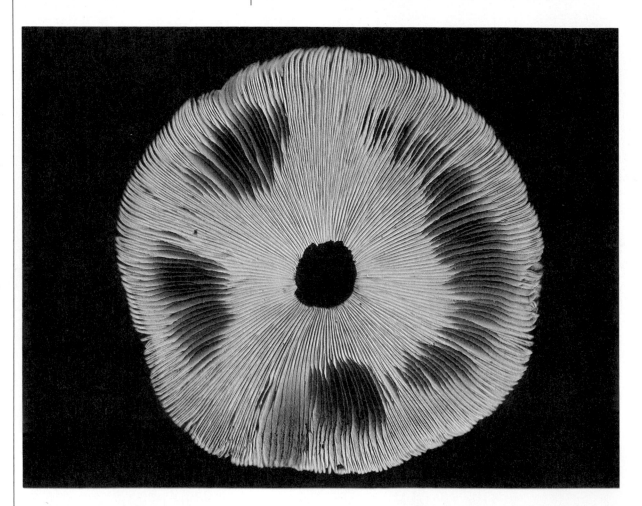

This is a print of the bottom of a mushroom cap. The white spores show up on the dark paper.

carried almost everywhere by moving air. There are spores of mushrooms and molds in your home. Usually you do not find mushrooms growing there. But mold spores can grow almost anywhere in your home. How can mold start growing on wrapped bread?

Fungi need water to grow. There are many places in your home that are **moist.** A moist place is where there is water. The inside of a refrigerator is usually moist. Most fresh fruits and vegetables are moist. Cake and bread can get moist. Towels and washcloths may be wet for a long time. Water pipes and tanks may have water on the outside. Basement walls and floors may also be moist. Fungi can get enough water to grow in all these places. Where might fungi grow in your home?

Fungi do not grow in all moist places. They can grow only where they can also get food. They need energy from food. Remember that fungi use plant and animal material for food. Which moist places in your home would have food for fungi?

Sometimes fungi grow where they are not expected. They grow on materials that do not seem to be food. Some of these materials are metal, glass, cement, and plastic. **Mildew** (mil′dü) is a kind of fungi. It often grows on water pipes and other moist places. You may have seen it in a shower. What could mildew use for food in these places?

TRY THIS

Use what you have learned to hunt for fungi. Search for mold and mildew in your home. Mold looks like fuzz. Mildew makes black or gray stains where it grows. List the places where you find mold or mildew.

1. What is one thing that fungi need in order to grow?

Checking What You Learned

USING SCIENCE WORDS

You learned some new science words in this unit. Some of them are listed in column B below. Write the numbers 1 – 5 on a sheet of paper. Read the phrases in column A. Decide which word in column B best matches each phrase in column A. Write the correct word next to each number on your paper. (You need not use all the words listed in column B.)

A	B
1. Adding water to crops	dodder
2. Nongreen plants having no roots, stems, or leaves	mildew
	penicillin
	microscope
3. Fungi grow from these small plant parts	fungi
	spores
4. A kind of fungi	irrigation
5. A mold product used to fight disease	

CHECKING THE FACTS

Write the numbers 1 – 5 on a sheet of paper. Then read the sentences below. Decide whether each one is true or false. If it is true, write <u>T</u> next to the number. If it is false, write <u>F</u>.

1. Starch is made by nongreen plants.

2. Most vegetables and flowers are grown from seeds.

3. Hundreds of small plants can live in a single drop of water.

4. Fungi get their food from trapped sunlight.

5. Some plants get their food from other plants or from animals.

ACTIVITIES TO TRY

1. Make a list of some plants that are grown in Alaska and Hawaii. Which of the plants are used as food? Why can some be grown in Hawaii but not in Alaska?

2. Choose 2 healthy houseplants. They should be as much alike as possible. Put them on a window-sill in your classroom. Cover one plant with a sheet of blue cellophane. Leave the other one uncovered. Make sure they each get the same amount of sunlight. Water them each day.

After a few days, remove the blue cellophane from the covered plant. Study both plants. How are they alike? How are they different? Do you think the same thing would happen if you used clear cellophane? Try using a sheet of red or yellow cellophane.

Keep a record of what you see during this activity. Ask the school librarian to help you find books on plants and light. This will help you explain some of your findings.

IDEAS TO THINK ABOUT

1. Plants need sunlight and water to make food. How do desert plants live without much rainfall? How can some plants live in swamps? Do you think green plants could live inside a cave? Give reasons for your answers.

2. Nongreen plants cannot make their own food. They get their food from dead plant and animal matter. How do nongreen plants help build up soil? Why are nongreen plants important? Go to the reference section of your library. List as many drugs made from nongreen plants as you can find.

SCIENCE AND YOU

Plants are important to us in many ways. They even provide people with jobs. Grocers sell the fruits and vegetables that farmers grow. Florists raise many kinds of plants in greenhouses. Foresters look after trees like the redwoods discussed on page 69. What other "plant" jobs can you name?

4

Health

Suppose you are walking home. A friend sees you. Your friend asks, "How are you?" What does your friend want to know?

How do you feel when you have done one of the following things?

Won a race

Written a good story

Been to a great party

Done some work that adults usually do

Each of those things is an activity. You move or think when you do activities. Most people feel good when they can do activities well.

People feel best when they are healthy. Healthy people work well. Healthy people have fun when they play. People who want to feel good must try to be healthy.

Is he "out," or "safe"? How do games like this help you stay healthy?

1

Feeling Good

What must be put in an automobile before it will run? You are right if you said gasoline. Why must a toaster be plugged in to work? It must have electricity to work. Gasoline and electricity both supply energy. Energy is needed for things to move or change.

You get energy from food. You do not need much energy to sit or stand. Much more energy is needed to move around. Would you use more energy in science class or on the playground?

There is more energy in some foods than in others. Foods with starch and sugar have a lot of energy. Cereals and grain have a lot of starch. Flour is made from wheat. Wheat is a grain. Bread, cake, and cookies are made from flour.

1. What is energy needed for?

What is this man carrying? What probably happened here? Does your body ever "run out of gas"? How do you feel then?

Cycling uses up much energy.

Why is eating too many snacks not healthful?

You get energy from all these foods. Sweet foods also give you lots of energy. Candy, soda, and ice cream are sweet foods. Sometimes people can get more energy than they need from sweet foods. Most vegetables do not have much starch or sugar. They have other things a person needs to be healthy.

Fats and oils are foods with much energy. Meat, milk, nuts, butter, and margarine contain fats and oils. Everyone needs to eat some fats and oils. But many people eat more of these foods than they need.

Activity 19

Running

Swimming

Riding bike

Walking

Sawing wood

Housepainting
Carpentry

Dusting

Ironing

Standing Reading Writing

Sitting

Which activities use the most energy?

You need:

Metric ruler

A. Look at the graph. It shows the energy used for different activities. You can compare the amount of energy used for the different activities.

B. The energy you use is measured in **Calories** (kal′ər ēz). Each bar stands for the number of Calories used per hour. Find the number of Calories needed for sawing wood. Do this by using a metric ruler. Find the "0" mark on the ruler. Put it on the left end of the bar. Look at the right end of the bar. It is closest to the number 5 on the ruler. Each number on the ruler stands for 100 Calories. Therefore, 500 Calories would be needed to saw wood for an hour.

C. Measure the other bars.

Answer these:

1. Which activity takes the most energy?
2. Which activities can you do with less than 100 Calories?
3. How many Calories are needed to walk for an hour?
4. Which activities take more energy than walking?
5. Which activities might you do after school?
6. When do you use the most energy?

103

ALL SYSTEMS GO

You could ride a bike with a flat tire. A tire is only one part of a bike. All other parts would work as they should. Could you win a race with a flat tire? Could you ride a bike if its chain broke? Is every part of a bicycle as important as every other part?

Your body is something like a bicycle. It is made of many parts. In a healthy body, all parts work as they should. Some parts of the body are more important than others. You cannot live if some parts are not working. Other parts are not as important. You may not do things well when those parts are not working. Or you may just feel sick. What are some of the most important parts of your body? Which parts can you live without?

Different parts of your body work together. Your teeth work with your stomach. They both work to change food. Your stomach works best when food is in small pieces. How would losing your teeth affect your stomach?

You may think that you walk using only your legs. But other parts of your body do help you walk. You feel things with nerves in your skin. Could you walk if you could not feel things? Your feet would touch the floor and you wouldn't know it. Parts of your ears also help you

It is difficult to tie your shoes when you have a broken arm. But he'll do it.

walk. There are small tubes inside your ears. These tubes are filled with a liquid. The liquid in these tubes helps you keep your balance. What happens when you turn around fast? The liquid moves. This makes you feel dizzy. It is hard to walk when you are dizzy. Do your eyes help you walk? Find out. Close your eyes and try to walk a straight line.

Have you ever gone to a carnival or fair? If you have, you may have taken a ride like this. You may have felt dizzy when you got off. What happened in your ears?

Activity 20

How well can you work without one of your senses?

You need:

3 milk cartons (bottom halves)	Clock
25 large nails	Paper
25 small nails	Pencil

A. There are nails of two sizes in the box. Your job is to sort the nails. The small nails will be put in one empty box. The large nails will be put in the other. Write the time on a piece of paper. Now start sorting. Check the time again when you have finished sorting. Find out how many minutes it takes to sort the nails.

B. Now suppose you closed your eyes. You could still sort nails. But would it be harder than with your eyes open? Mix the nails together in one box. Record the time. Close your eyes. Keep them closed until you have sorted the nails. How long did it take?

Answer these:

1. In step **A** you sorted nails with your eyes open. How long did it take?
2. How much longer did it take with your eyes closed?
3. List 5 things that would be hard to do with your eyes closed.

LITTLE THINGS CAN HURT

Think about the sounds you hear in a schoolroom. Some sounds are heard almost every day. There are the sounds of people moving. There are sounds of people talking. There are sounds of the pencil sharpener being used. People make sounds when they write. Chairs, tables, and desks make sounds when they are used. You could think of these as sounds of health. Healthy people make sounds as they work and play.

The girl is having a checkup. Why is the doctor looking in the girl's mouth?

2. What is a symptom? Give some symptoms of a cold.

You may also hear sounds of sickness in your classroom. A cough is such a sound. In almost every classroom someone has a cold. A cough is a **symptom** (simp′ təm) of a cold. A symptom is a sign. There are other symptoms of colds. Stuffy heads, runny noses, and red eyes are symptoms. There is one symptom that cannot be heard or seen. A person with a cold does not feel well. This may be the first symptom of catching a cold. What does "catching a cold" mean?

A cold is a disease. Mumps, chicken pox, and flu are also diseases. What other diseases can you name?

There are symptoms for all diseases. A symptom of mumps is swelling under the ears. Red spots on the skin are a symptom of chicken pox. A **fever** (fe′ vər) is a symptom of flu. A fever is a higher than usual temperature. A fever is a symptom of many diseases. So is "not feeling well."

Suppose you do not feel well for a few days. You have a symptom of a disease. You may go to the doctor to be checked. The doctor or nurse may check your temperature. The doctor may then look for other symptoms. The doctor may know the disease from your symptoms.

More than one disease may have the same symptoms. A doctor cannot always be certain of what disease you have. If the disease is serious, more checks will be

This scientist is studying the cause of one disease—cancer. We cannot try to prevent a disease until we know what causes it.

made. A sample of your blood may be checked. A sample of the liquid in your mouth may also be checked. What are doctors looking for in these samples?

Colds, mumps, and chickenpox are caused by tiny **germs.** Some germs are living; some are not. **Bacteria** (bak tir′ ē ə) are living germs. **Viruses** (vī′ r ə sez) are not alive. Bacteria and viruses are too small to be seen with the eyes alone. Microscopes must be used to see them.

Many kinds of germs can live in your body. They may be in your blood. Or they may be in other body liquids. Each kind of germ causes a certain disease. The doctor may find a certain germ in your body. The doctor can tell what disease you have by knowing what the germ is.

Not feeling well is a symptom. It may mean there are germs in your body. Then you should take special care of yourself. You should tell a parent or teacher how you feel. You should make sure that you get enough sleep. If the feeling lasts, you should visit a doctor.

These are molds growing on agar in a petri dish. Penicillin comes from these molds. What is penicillin used for?

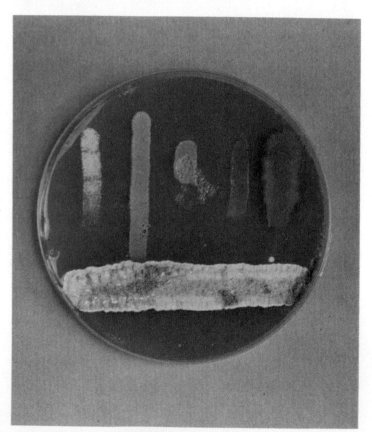

Activity 21

What diseases have you had?

You need:

Pencil
Paper
Metric ruler

A. Draw lines on paper as shown in the drawing. Use a metric ruler to make the lines straight. Write the word Disease at the top of the left-hand column. Write Have Had in the middle column. Write Immunized in the column at the right.

DISEASE	HAVE HAD	IMMU-NIZED
CHICKEN POX		
DIPHTHERIA		
IMPETIGO		
INFLUENZA (FLU)		
MEASLES		
MUMPS		
POLIOMYELITIS (POLIO)		
SMALLPOX		
TETANUS		
TYPHOID FEVER		
WHOOPING COUGH		

B. Copy the list of diseases. Put a check mark (✔) in the column that applies to each disease. Check Have Had if you have had the disease. Check Immunized if you have been immunized for the disease. **Immunized** (im' yü nized) means you have had shots for a disease. You may ask a parent to help you complete your disease record.

Answer these:

1. For which diseases have you been immunized?
2. Which diseases did you need shots for before starting school? Find out if you are not sure.

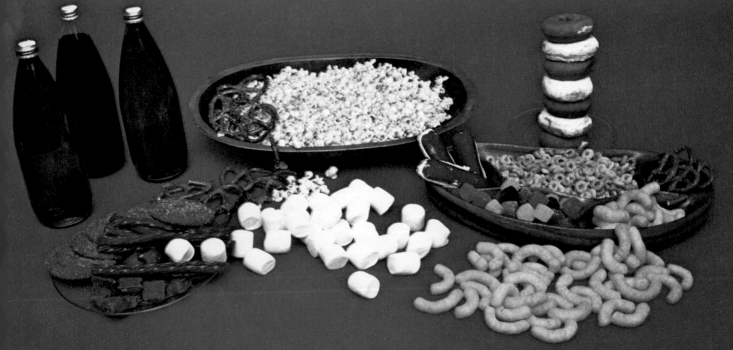

Good Habits for Good Health

Do you watch television after school or on Saturdays? If you do, you are told what foods you should eat. You are also told why you should eat them. One cereal is to be eaten because of its shape. Another, because it is crunchy. Still another comes with toys in the package. There are also commercials for hamburgers and fried chicken. You are supposed to eat at one place because "Mom" needs a break. You are to eat at another because "kids get balloons." You should eat somewhere else because "Dad will like it." Are these the real reasons for eating foods?

Besides energy, your body needs materials to grow. You get these materials by eating food. These materials are called **nutrients** (nü′ trē ∂ntz). The real reason for eating is to get nutrients.

It is easy to see which of these "meals" has junk food. Junk foods taste good. But they don't give you nutrients like those in the meal in the top picture.

No one food has all the nutrients you need. You must eat many kinds of foods to get them. What you eat is called your **diet** (dī ət). A good diet will give you all the nutrients you need.

You have already read about your need for energy. You learned that starch, sugar, fats, and oils supply energy. Starch, sugar, fats, and oils are nutrients. Foods with those nutrients should be in your diet. Can you name some examples of those foods?

Protein (prō′ tēn) is a nutrient your body needs for growth. Protein is also needed to repair worn-out parts. Your muscles are made mainly of protein. You can get proteins by eating meat. Other foods with proteins are milk, eggs, beans, and nuts. There are many kinds of protein. Your body needs more than one kind. You can get the different kinds by eating different foods. Proteins also supply energy. Why would eating only hamburgers be a poor diet?

Your body needs fats and oils. The body can use fats and oils for energy. But it does not need them for energy. You can get most of your energy from other foods. Fats and oils supply some **vitamins** (vī′ tə minz) that you need. Vitamins are chemicals that keep your body working.

There are many kinds of vitamins. The vitamins are named by letters. The most

Your body needs vitamins to stay healthy. Vitamins are in the food you eat. Some people do not get all their vitamins from food. They buy vitamin pills like those shown here.

common vitamins are those named A, B, C, D, E, and K. There are also vitamins B_1, B_2, B_3, B_6, and B_{12}.

Almost all foods contain some vitamins. Some foods have a lot of one vitamin. They may have none of the others. You should get some of each vitamin every day. You get them by eating many kinds of food. A good diet gives a person all the vitamins needed. Vitamin pills are not needed by people with a good diet.

The body also needs **minerals** (min′ ər əlz). Minerals are chemicals used in growing body parts. Minerals in milk form strong bones and teeth. Liver, molasses, and green vegetables all have one important mineral—iron. Iron is needed for blood. A growing body needs much food that contains minerals.

Too much of one kind of food makes a poor diet. Too much of some vitamins can make a person sick. Too much sugar causes tooth decay. Extra sugar also makes a person fat. Most Americans eat too much fat and oil. Fats and oils can make a person overweight. They can also cause diseases of the blood, heart, and liver.

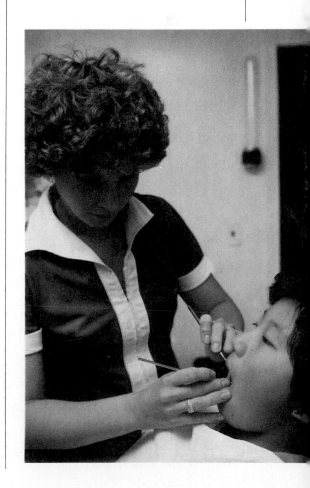

Calcium is a mineral. It is found in many foods. There is a rich supply of calcium in milk. Calcium is needed for strong, healthy teeth.

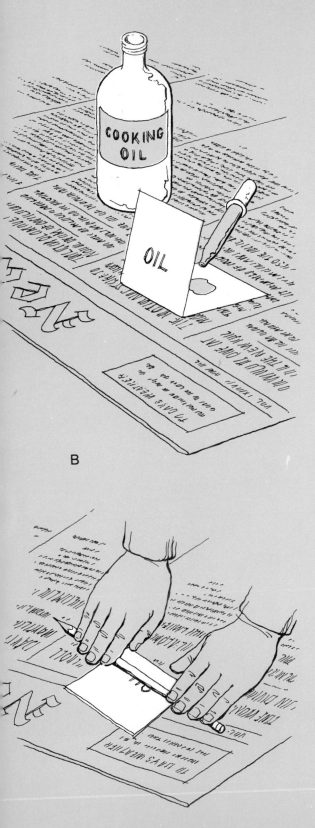

B

Activity 22

Which of your snack foods contain much fat or oil?

You need:
Pieces of brown wrapping paper
Pieces of 5 or more different snack foods
Water
Cooking oil
Margarine
Pencil
Paper towels
Newspaper
Medicine dropper

A. Put a newspaper on your desk top or table. Do all your work on the newspaper.

B. Fold a piece of the wrapping paper in half. Write the word Oil on the paper. Put one drop of cooking oil inside the folded paper. Close the paper. Roll a pencil over the outside of the paper. How does oil change the paper? Wipe the pencil with a paper towel.

C. Do the same thing with margarine. Use only a very small amount of margarine. Wipe the pencil with a paper towel.

D. Do the same thing with a drop of water. Wipe the pencil with a paper towel.

E. Make the same test with 5 or more kinds of snack foods. Use only small bits of the foods. Wipe the pencil with a paper towel after each test.

F. Look at the papers on which you put oil, margarine, and water. One of the papers has changed since you first looked at it. Which paper is it?

Answer these:

1. Which snack foods contained much oil or fat?
2. Which snack foods did not contain much oil or fat?
3. What happens to a water spot after a long while?
4. How do you know that water in snack foods did not change the papers?

117

YOUR BODY CATCHES UP

Do you have to go to bed at a certain time? Most people of your age do. The time is usually set by an adult. Have you ever wondered why people sleep? Why do babies sleep so much? Why do children have to go to bed before adults do? The activity on the next page may give you clues to the answers.

What makes your muscles feel tired? Muscles need energy to work. The energy comes from sugar in your blood. Waste materials form as sugar is used. Blood carries these waste materials from your muscles.

You use a lot of energy when you skate. You use many muscles. You probably feel tired after you skate.

Activity 23

What happens when your fingers work for a long time without resting?

You need:
Clock with a sweep-second hand

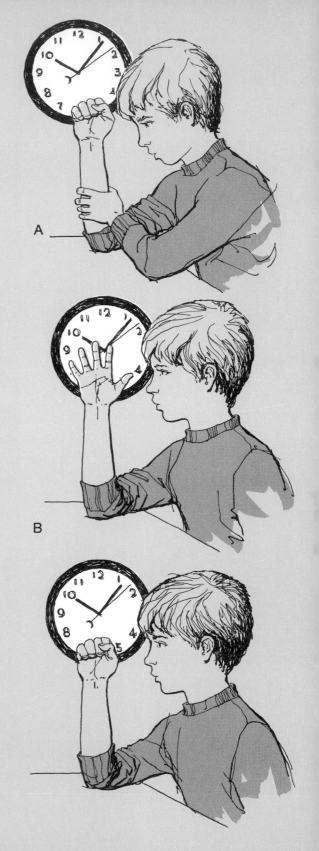

A. Muscles in your arm move your fingers. Slowly open and close the fingers of your right hand. Feel the muscles in your lower arm move. These are the muscles that move your fingers.

B. Raise your right hand. Check the time. Open and close the fingers of your right hand as fast as you can. Do this until the muscles in your arm start to ache. Stop. Check the time when you stop. How long could you move your fingers before the muscles ached?

C. Rest your hand and arm for one minute.

D. After a minute, do step **B** again.

Answer these:

1. How long could you open and close your fingers in step **B?**

2. How long could you open and close your fingers after a 1-minute rest?

3. Did your muscles tire sooner the second time you did step **B?** Why?

4. Suppose you had rested 10 minutes instead of 1 minute. How might this have changed your answer to question **2?**

Much waste material forms when muscles work long or hard. Your blood cannot remove the waste as quickly as it forms. The waste collects in your muscles. It is really a weak poison. This poison makes your muscles feel tired. If still more waste collects, your muscles stop working. Which of those things happened to you?

All parts of your body use energy when they work. Waste collects in nearly all parts of your body. There are many wastes in your body at day's end. Your body needs time to get rid of those wastes.

3. Why is sleep important to your body?

Most parts of your body work more slowly when you sleep. While you sleep, you use less energy. Your body gets rid of wastes while you sleep. Sleep gives parts of your body time to rest.

YOUR NEEDS CHANGE

Think of all the things you did yesterday. You dressed and ate. You may have gone to school. Most people your age play games. Did you? You did some reading, thinking, and writing. You probably walked, talked, ran, and shouted. Does a baby do the kinds of things you did?

What kinds of things does a baby do? Does an adult do the same things you do? What different kinds of things do adults do?

You do work as your body grows and changes. A person grows at different rates at different times. You grew fast during the first year of your life. A baby more than doubles its weight in a year. So a baby needs a lot of food. Babies also need a lot of sleep. They may sleep 18 to 20 hours a day. Young babies must be kept warm. A baby must have much care in its first year. Suppose you were growing as fast as a baby. How much would you weigh next year?

A baby's head is large in comparison with the baby's total size. An adult's legs are long in comparison with the adult's total size. What other body changes do you notice?

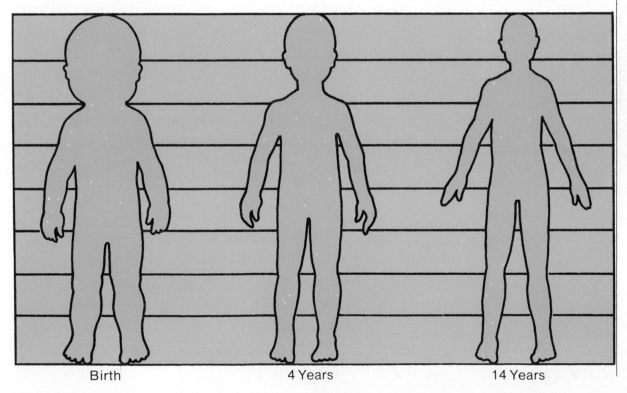

Birth   4 Years   14 Years

4. There are two times in your life when you grow very fast. When are they?

Children between one and twelve do not grow as fast as babies. You are in this age group. You will not double your weight this year. For your size, you do not eat as much as a baby eats. You also need less sleep than a baby needs. Children in this age group should sleep 10 to 14 hours. At your age you can do many things for yourself. But children do not always know what is best for them. At those times, they need advice from older people.

Most people begin to grow faster again at about age twelve. Their adult bodies take shape during their teenage years. Most people eat more during those years. But they are not as active as most people your age. Older teenagers spend more time sitting and talking than you do. They need less sleep. They may sleep only 7 to 9 hours a day.

Adults have stopped growing taller. But they may gain weight because they eat too much. They do not need energy to grow.

Most older people are not as active as younger people. They do not use as much energy for movement. Most people eat less as they grow older. Older people usually need less sleep. An older person may sleep only 5 to 7 hours a day. How would you feel if you had only this much sleep each night?

Activity 24

How much sleep do you get?

You need:

Pencil   Paper   Metric ruler

A. Make a record sheet like the one in the diagram.

B. Record the times you go to bed and wake up. Figure out how long you have slept. Do this each day for 7 days.

C. Find the total number of hours you slept in the week.

D. You probably did not get the same amount of sleep each day. Most people sleep more on some days than on others. You might not have slept enough on some days. You may have made up for it on other days.

A person your age usually sleeps about 10 hours a day. This would be 70 hours a week. Compare the time you slept with the time you should have slept.

DAY	TIME TO BED	WOKE UP	HOURS SLEPT
1			
2			
3			
4			
5			
6			
7			
TOTAL			

Answer these:

1. How many days did you sleep less than 10 hours?

2. How many days did you sleep more than 10 hours?

3. Did you sleep more or less than 70 hours in the week?

4. Do you think you get enough sleep?

FIGHTING WITH SOAP

Suppose you get enough food and sleep. To stay healthy, you must keep germs from your body. If you don't, you will get a disease. You will have lost your good health.

Your body can fight most germs that cause disease. It can make chemicals that will kill germs. There are also cells in your body that destroy germs. You get well when germs are destroyed. But you are sick while your body battles them.

It is best to keep germs out of your body. To do this, you battle germs outside of the body. Most germs cause harm only when they are growing and multiplying. You can win your battle by keeping them from growing.

Germs are almost everywhere. Fighting them would be easier if they could be seen. But knowing about them helps fight them. You know that most germs are living things. They need the same things other living things need. They need food and water.

Germs must be touching the food they use. They must be moist to grow. Dirt has both food and the moisture that germs need. Most dirty places are places where germs can live. Germs do not grow well where it is clean.

Germs travel in the air. That is why you should cover your mouth when you sneeze.

Germs probably grow well here. One way to get rid of the germs is to clean up the litter.

The body is a dirt collector. Skin is nearly always moist from sweat. Sweat is mostly water and salt. The skin also gives off oil. Dirt is held on the skin by sweat and oil. Some germs use the sweat and oil for food. Why do your fingers leave prints on things you touch?

Washing the skin gets rid of most dirt. This takes away materials that germs use for food. Some parts of your body are harder to clean than others. Dirt under fingernails is hard to wash away. Hair can hold much dirt.

Clothing and dishes can be washed cleaner than skin. They can be washed in very hot water. Germs can be killed with very hot water. Water hot enough to kill germs will burn skin. Strong chemicals can also be used to clean these things. Most bleaches used on clothing kill germs. But bleaches can be dangerous. They can burn the eyes and skin. They are also poisonous.

Skin is one of the body's best defenses against disease. But if the skin is dirty, it is like a street with litter. Why?

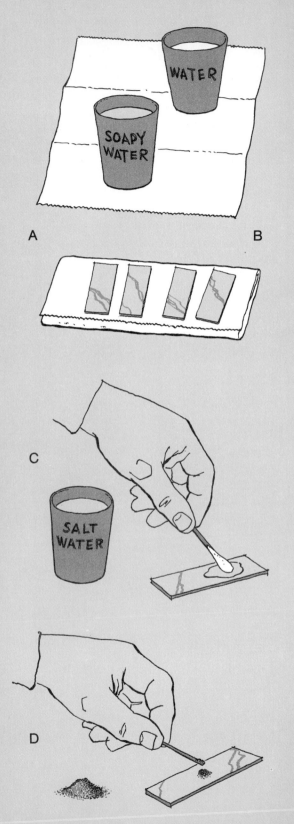

A

B

C

D

Activity 25

Why is soap or detergent used?

You need:

4 microscope slides	Toothpick
Dry soil	Cotton swabs
Cooking oil	Paper towels
Salt water	3 plastic tumblers
Soap or detergent solution	Water

A. Spread 2 clean paper towels on your desk or table. One towel will be used only for microscope slides. Do all other work on the other towel.

B. Check the slides to see if they are clean. Look through each slide, toward a light. If you see any dirt on a slide, get a clean one. Put the clean slides on one of the towels. Nearly fill one tumbler with clean water. Nearly fill the other with soap or detergent solution. Put the tumblers on the other paper towel.

C. Dip a cotton swab in salt water. Rub the swab over one end of a microscope slide. Move the slide to the top of the paper towel. The salt water will dry while you work with other slides.

D. Get some dry soil on the end of a toothpick. Put the soil on one end of another slide. Pick up the slide by its edges. Put the dirty end of the slide in the glass of water.

Move it back and forth 5 times. Look for dirt on the slide.

E. Dip a cotton swab in oil. Rub oil on one end of a slide. Sprinkle some soil on the oil. Put the dirty end of the slide in the glass of water. Move it back and forth 5 times. Look for dirt on the slide. If you see any dirt, dip it in the soap or detergent solution. Move the slide back and forth 5 times. Then dip it in water again. Look for dirt on the slide.

F. Press a fingertip on another slide. Try to wash the print off in water. Then see if it will wash off in the soap or detergent solution.

G. The salt water should have dried on the first slide. You should see spots of salt on the glass. Find out if the salt will wash off with only water.

Answer these:

1. What could be washed from the slides with water?

2. What could not be washed from the slides without soap or detergent?

E

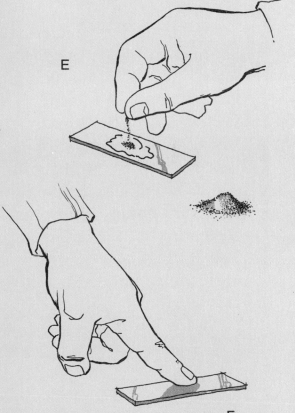

E

F

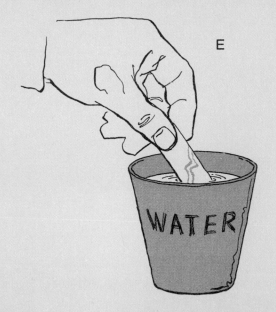

E

Checking What You Learned

USING SCIENCE WORDS

You learned some new science words in this unit. Some of them are listed in column B below. Write the numbers 1−6 on a sheet of paper. Read the phrases in column A. Decide which word in column B best matches each phrase in column A. Write the correct word next to each number on your paper. (You need not use all the words listed in column B.)

A	B
1. The amount of energy in food	bacteria
2. Sugars and starches	calories
3. A sign of disease	carbohydrates
4. Nutrients that help build bones and teeth	germ
5. A, B$_1$, B$_2$, C, and K are some.	immunize
6. A nutrient that helps build body tissues	minerals
	nutrients
	protein
	symptom
	vitamins

CHECKING THE FACTS

Write the numbers 1−6 on a sheet of paper. Then read the sentences below. Decide whether each one is true or false. If it is true, write T next to the number. If it is false, write F.

1. You get energy from the food you eat.
2. Carbohydrates do not have much energy.
3. A sick person often has a high fever or high body temperature.
4. Penicillin is a virus.
5. Snack foods have many nutrients.
6. Bacteria and viruses are kinds of germs.

ACTIVITIES TO TRY

1. Keep track of all the food you eat for three days. Get a Calorie counter. Add up the number of Calories you ate each day. Which foods are highest in Calories? Which are lowest?

Look at your list. Did you eat any junk foods? If so, what were were they?

2. Bring in many different kinds of empty food containers. Ask your parents to save them for you. You might collect empty cereal boxes, egg cartons, and fruit and vegetable cans. (Be sure to wash out the cans before bringing them to school.) Look at the labels on the containers. Many of them tell the kinds of nutrients the food contains. Group the containers according to the main kind of nutrient they list. Put high-protein foods together. Put carbohydrates together. Put fats and oils together. Make signs to describe your display.

IDEAS TO THINK ABOUT

1. Many years ago, children often died when they were very young. What reasons can you give for this? What things helped you grow up to be strong and healthy?
2. Many adults are on diets. They are usually trying to lose weight. What kinds of foods should people on diets eat? What kinds of foods should they not eat? People on diets often take vitamin pills. Why is this important?

SCIENCE AND YOU

You have only one body. So people must take care of it. There are many jobs in health care. You probably think right away of doctors, nurses, and dentists. But there are many other jobs in the health field. Hospitals need laboratory technicians, cooks, and cleaning people, too. Any job in the health field can be important and interesting.

Matter All Around You

Have you ever played the game "What do I work with?" Suppose you were a baker. What would you work with? You probably thought right away of dough and pans and ovens. What about a carpenter? Again, you probably had no trouble. Maybe you thought of wood and tools.

Now, what about a scientist? What does a scientist work with? Did you think of test tubes, or powders, or germs? If you did, you would be only partly right. A scientist works with **matter.** Everything that has weight and takes up space is matter. This book, your desk, the school bus—even you yourself! Everything is made of matter.

There are many sights, sounds, and odors at this 4-H Club fair. What things in the picture are matter?

The States of Matter

All matter can be found in three **states,** or forms. Matter can be a **solid,** a **liquid,** or a **gas.** A solid has a fixed size and shape. It may be big, like a large rock. Or it may be powdery, like sand or sugar. All liquids have a fixed size but no fixed shape. Liquids take the shape of their containers.

Some matter is not a solid or a liquid. It is a gas. A gas does not have a fixed size or shape. Gases are sometimes hard to notice because they are invisible.

What kind of matter is perfume? Is it a solid, a liquid, or a gas? When you smell perfume, fried chicken, or a skunk, you smell a gas. Water vapor is a gas. Can you smell water vapor? Air is a mixture of gases. Can you smell air? Most gases do not have an odor.

How are these forms of matter alike? How are they different?

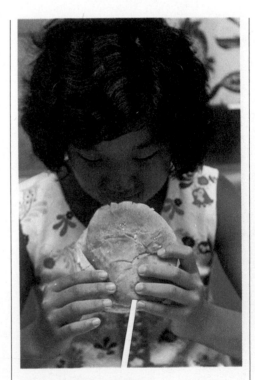

This girl is changing the size and shape of solid matter.

Activity 26

How long does ice last?

You need:

5 paper cups	Cool water
5 ice cubes	Hot water
Clock or watch	Marking pen
Refrigerator	

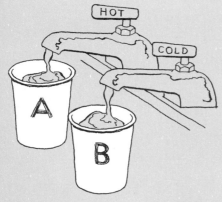

A. Mark your cups A, B, C, D, and E. Put 1 ice cube in each cup.

B. Half fill cup A with hot tap water. Half fill cup B with cool tap water. Don't put any water in cups C, D, and E.

C. Put cups A, B, and C on your desk. Put cup D in the refrigerator. Put cup E in the freezer of the refrigerator. What do you think will happen to each cube?

D. Check each cup in 10 minutes. Check them at the end of your science lesson. Check them again at the end of the day.

Answer these:

1. Were the guesses you made in step **C** correct?

2. If you were wrong, can you tell why?

3. If the cubes changed, why did they change?

Activity 27

Where is the perfume?

You need:

5 paper cups
Perfume
5 small pieces of cotton
5 small pieces of cloth
5 rubber bands
Marking pen
Water
Medicine dropper

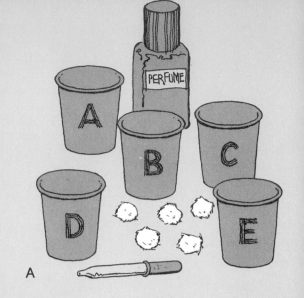

A

A. Label your cups A, B, C, D, and E.

B. Put a small piece of cotton in each cup. Put 5 drops of perfume on one piece of cotton. Put 5 drops of water on each of the other pieces of cotton.

C. Cover each cup with a small piece of cloth, as shown. Hold the cloth in place with a rubber band.

D. Put the 5 cups on your desk. Have some of your classmates try to find the perfume cup. Don't let them touch your cups!

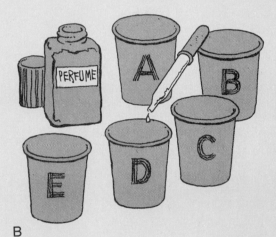

B

Answer these:

1. Could your classmates find out which cup contained the perfume?

2. Why was water put in the other cups?

3. How did the perfume get to the people you tested?

4. How long will it take you to locate the cup with perfume.

C

135

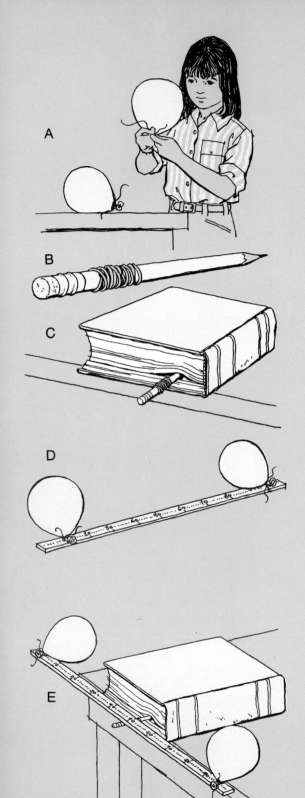

A

B

C

D

E

Activity 28

Does gas have weight?

You need:

2 medium-sized balloons	Masking tape
Meterstick	String
Pencil (round)	Pin
Large book	Rubber band

A. Blow up each balloon about the same size. Tie it closed with a piece of string.

B. Wind a rubber band around the pencil.

C. Put a thick book on the edge of a table. It should stick out over the edge of the table. Put the pencil between the pages of the book.

D. Tape the string holding each balloon to each end of the meterstick.

E. Balance the meterstick with the balloons on the pencil. Use the rubber band to keep the meterstick from sliding.

F. Guess which way the meterstick will swing if you pop one of the balloons. Then pop one balloon with a pin.

Answer these:

1. Which way did the meterstick swing? Did you guess correctly?

2. Why did the meterstick swing the way it did?

3. Does air have weight? Explain your answer.

Look at the picture below. How many different solids and liquids do you see? Can you see gases?

All three forms of matter are found here. This is Pilot Ridge in the Northern Cascade Mountains in Washington State.

When water becomes a gas, you cannot see it. It is called **water vapor** (vā′pər). Most of the small drops of liquid water in the air will turn into water vapor. Then you will not see them.

At what time of year was this picture probably taken? How can you tell? Would the ice cream melt faster or slower on white concrete than it does here? Explain.

Look at the picture on this page. You have seen ice cream melt. Ice cream is a solid. It changes to a liquid when it melts. What causes this change? What else do you know that changes from a solid to a liquid? Can you think of anything that changes from a liquid to a solid?

Many materials can change from one form to another—solid, liquid, or gas. This is called **change of state.** Matter changes state by taking in or giving off heat.

Activity 29

What things will change from liquids to solids in a freezer?

You need:
Graduated cylinder
5 paper cups
Thermometer
Marking pen
Refrigerator
Any 5 of these liquids:

Water	Salt water
Syrup	Rubbing alcohol
Milk	(Be sure to use this.)
Vinegar	Liquid bleach
Soda pop	Cooking oil

A. Put 25 mL of each liquid into a clean paper cup. Write the name on the cup.
B. Check the temperature of each liquid. Wipe off your thermometer after you put it into each liquid.
C. Put the cups in the freezer.
D. Check the temperature in each cup at the end of class. Check it again at the end of the day.

Answer these:
1. What changes took place in the cups? Did any of the liquids change to solids? Did any stay liquid? Which ones?
2. What happened to the temperature of each liquid during the day?

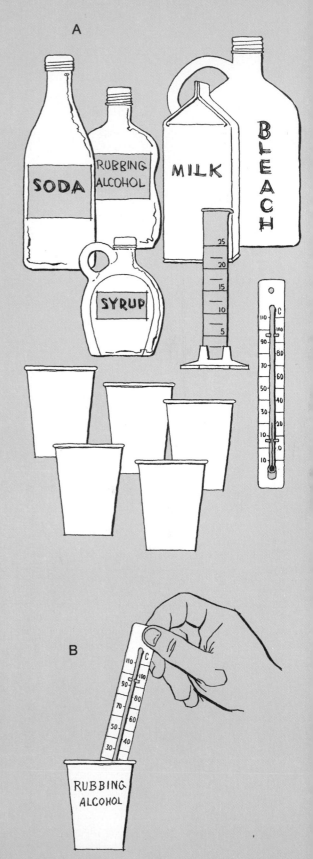

Physical and Chemical Changes

As ice melts, a **physical change** takes place. A liquid changing to a solid is another physical change. So are liquids changing to gases, or gases changing to liquids. All these physical changes are changes of state. A physical change may affect the way something looks. But that "something" is still the same thing.

A change of state is only one kind of physical change. There are other kinds. Suppose you break a stick in two. Is this a physical change? Why? Did you change the state of the stick? Did you change the stick into something else? What other physical changes can you think of?

Chemicals on this sparkler give off light when they burn. New chemicals are formed. This is a chemical change. What kind of change is shown by the child breaking the stick?

How small can matter be? How small can you make something? You can break a stick into many small pieces. You can grind a piece of chalk into dust. But dust is made up of things smaller than you can see. Scientists call these tiny, basic units **atoms** and **molecules** (mol′ ə kyüls). Millions of molecules make up the tiniest speck of dust. Atoms and molecules cannot be seen even with the most powerful microscopes (mī′ krə skōps). All matter is made of tiny atoms or molecules.

TRY THIS
How small can you get? Tear a piece of paper the size of a postage stamp into tiny pieces. Keep tearing until you can tear no more. How many pieces of paper did you get? Did you change the paper into something else? What kind of change took place in the paper?

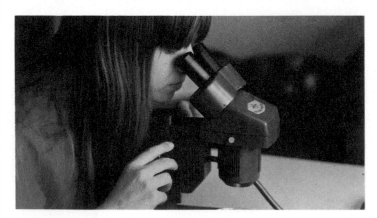

Can this girl see the atoms and molecules in the leaf? What does she see?

When you did **Try This,** you made many tiny pieces of paper. Yet even the smallest piece had millions of molecules. In some of the other activities, you did many things to matter. You added heat. You took away heat. All these things changed matter. You changed the size, shape, and state of matter. All these changes are physical changes.

Physical changes do not change what a substance is made of. Clay is still clay after you mold it and shape it. Sugar is still sugar after you stir it into water. How can you tell that the sugar is still there? Water is still water when it is ice. Energy is used in all these physical changes. Often this energy is in the form of heat. When does heat cause a substance to change physically? Give some examples of such physical changes.

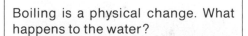

Boiling is a physical change. What happens to the water?

143

What made the cement crack? What made the fruit change? How are the changes different?

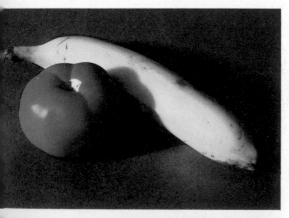

People may cause physical changes. But other living things also cause change. Have you ever seen a puppy tear a shoe apart? Cats sometimes sharpen their claws on chair legs. They also use their claws to tear away bits of food. Bears sharpen their claws on trees. Sometimes they tear away large pieces of bark. Even plants can cause physical change. Tree roots may grow in cracks in rocks. The growing roots may break up the rocks.

CHEMICAL CHANGE

Not all changes are physical changes. Sometimes new matter forms when matter changes. The new matter does not act like the old matter. It does not look like the old matter. It is a new kind of matter. A change like this is a **chemical change.**

Many chemical changes are useful. The food you eat must be chemically changed. Then your body can use it. The chemical change of food gives your body energy.

Other chemical changes are not useful. Sometimes food that is kept too long spoils. This is also a chemical change.

Chemical changes may take place when two kinds of matter are mixed. Parts of the two kinds of matter join together. A new kind of matter is formed when this happens. The new matter is not like the matter from which it was formed.

Activity 30

How can you form new matter?

You need:

Baking soda	Graduated cylinder
Vinegar	(or metric cup)
Spoon	Round balloon
Empty soft-drink bottle	Funnel

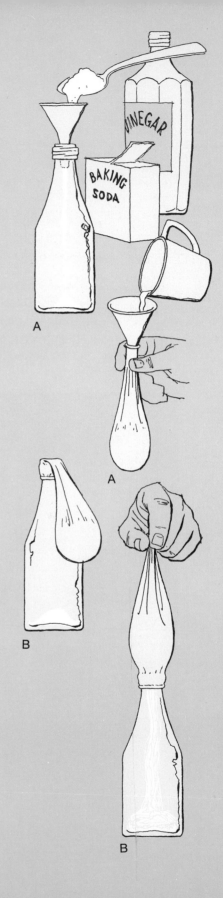

A. Put a funnel in the mouth of the soft-drink bottle. Put 15 mL of baking soda in the soft-drink bottle. Put 50 mL of vinegar in the balloon.

B. Put the open end of the balloon over the top of the bottle. Lift the end of the balloon. Make sure the vinegar goes into the bottle. Watch what happens.

C. Take the balloon off the bottle when the bubbling stops. Add another 15 mL of baking soda.

Answer these:

1. In which state was the baking soda when you began? In which state was the vinegar when you began?

2. What happened when vinegar and baking soda were mixed?

3. In which state of matter were the bubbles?

4. Was the vinegar still vinegar when you were done? Explain your answer.

5. Did a chemical change take place? Explain.

FIRE, HEAT, AND CHANGE

Fire can be dangerous. But fire can also be useful. It is useful because it gives heat. People use fire to keep warm. They also use it to change matter.

Fire can cause both physical and chemical changes. Heat is used to melt matter. It is used to boil matter. Metals are changed from a solid to a liquid with heat. All these are physical changes. Why are these changes in matter physical changes?

Oxygen is combining rapidly with the matter in this forest. How is burning like rusting? How is it different?

Fire also causes chemical changes. Do you like raw meat? It tastes better cooked. It is also easier to chew. Is cooking a chemical change? How do you know? Wood is heated in ovens to make charcoal. Garbage and waste are heated to make fertilizers. All these are chemical changes caused by heat.

TIME AND CHANGE

All matter is changing. Some changes happen very slowly. Sometimes no differences can be seen in a thousand years. Some rocks look the same today as they did long ago. Brick and many metals also change slowly.

But there are many kinds of rapid changes. Cloth and paper change rapidly if they are not protected. Burning materials change very rapidly. Some matter changes quickly when mixed with other matter. Baking soda and vinegar change quickly when mixed. Light causes chemical changes on the film in a camera. Light changes film in less than a second.

Living matter changes faster than most matter that is not alive. Living things change as they grow. Your body is warm because of fast chemical changes. You feel, move, touch, taste, and see because of chemical changes.

Rusting is a chemical change. During rusting, oxygen and moisture from the air combine with iron.

TRY THIS

Find out if iron can be changed chemically. Moisten a piece of steel wool with water. Put this into a clean baby-food jar. Put another piece of steel wool into another jar. Keep this wool dry. Do not put tops on the jars. Let the jars stand overnight. What happened to the steel wool in the jars? What kind of change was this? Is the new matter like the old matter? What caused this change?

Checking What You Learned

USING SCIENCE WORDS

You learned some important new science words in this unit. Write the numbers 1 – 5 on a sheet of paper. Then read the sentences below. After each number, write the word or phrase that correctly completes the sentence. Use these words: atoms, change of state, chemical change, gas, liquid, matter, molecules, physical change, solid, states, temperature, water vapor.

1. A state of matter that can be invisible is _____.

2. A change in the size or shape of matter is a _____.

3. Burning and rusting are examples of a _____.

4. There are three _____ of matter.

5. Matter is made of _____ and _____ that are too small to be seen with a microscope.

CHECKING THE FACTS

1. Write the letters **a – j** on a sheet of paper. Study the changes listed below. Decide which are chemical changes and which are physical changes. After each letter, write P if the change is a physical change. Write C if the change is a chemical change.

a. Burning wood
b. Chopping wood
c. Breaking glass
d. Mowing grass
e. Washing clothes
f. Sharpening a knife
g. Burning gasoline
h. Melting ice cream
i. Slicing bread
j. Baking bread

2. Write the letters **a – f** on a sheet of paper. Look at the kinds of matter listed below. Decide whether each is a solid, a liquid, or a gas. After each letter, write S if the matter is a solid. Write L if it is a liquid. Write G if it is a gas.

a. Snow
b. Oxygen
c. Clay
d. Paper
e. Steam
f. Ocean water

ACTIVITIES TO TRY

1. Cut some squares, circles, and other shapes from black construction paper. Put them on top of construction paper of a different color. Put the sheet of paper with the shapes on it in a sunny window. Leave it there for a few days. Then remove the black shapes. What do you see? Is there a change in the color of the sheet of paper? If so, is this a chemical or a physical change? Explain.

2. Lemon juice and vinegar are both weak acids. You can see a chemical change if you use them in this activity. Dip a toothpick into either lemon juice or vinegar. Using the toothpick, write a secret message on a piece of notebook paper. Let the writing dry. Can you see it now? Now hold the paper a few inches above a lighted candle. What happens? What caused the change? Can you think of another way to cause this change?

IDEAS TO THINK ABOUT

1. Do you live in the northern part of the United States? If you do, think about what it looks like in winter. What physical changes might you see? Which ones would you see in summer? Which would you not see? Do some physical changes take place in summer but not in winter? What are they?

2. Some physical and chemical changes are useful. Some are harmful. Make a list of some useful chemical and physical changes in your life. Make a list of some harmful chemical and physical changes. Compare your list with the lists of other pupils in your class.

SCIENCE AND YOU

Carpenters, cooks, dressmakers, and auto mechanics all change matter. So do artists and pharmacists. Can you name any jobs in which matter is not changed?

Making Work Easier

What is **work?** What kinds of work do you do? Did you know that you do work when you play tag?

You may think you work hard in school. You might say that arithmetic is "hard work." But a scientist would not agree. A scientist would say <u>you do work only when you move or you move something</u>. When you sit and think, you are not moving anything. So you are not working. But when you play tag, you move yourself. So you are doing work.

Work can be measured. To measure work, you must know how far something moves. You must also know how hard you push or pull the object. You will learn more about measuring work later on.

Moving to a new house takes a lot of work. This girl is getting some help from her new friends.

1

Kinds of Machines

What do you think when you hear the word <u>machine</u>? Perhaps you think of a giant bulldozer (bùl′ dō zər). Or you may think of factories or mills. But did you know that the classroom pencil sharpener is a machine? So is a screwdriver or a hammer. Machines may be big or little. Some machines are simple. Others are not. A **machine** is anything that helps you do work.

There are probably thousands of different machines in your community. But all machines are alike in certain ways. Every machine is made of one or more **simple machines.** There are six kinds of simple machines. They are the lever, wedge, screw, inclined plane, pulley, and wheel-and-axle.

1. How many kinds of simple machines are there?

This family is building their own house. It takes much work. What kinds of work are they doing here? What other kinds of work will they need to do?

THE LEVER

A **lever** (lev′ər) may be a bar, stick, or rod. It turns, or pivots (piv′əts), on a point. The point on which a lever turns is called the **fulcrum** (ful′krəm). In some levers, the fulcrum may be like a hinge. Scissors, shovels, crowbars, and bottle openers are levers. Look at the pictures of levers on this page. Find the fulcrum in each picture. Is the fulcrum always in the middle? Is it sometimes at one end? Put your finger on the fulcrum of each lever.

Levers are used to push, pull, or lift objects. The object moved is called the load, or **resistance** (ri zis′təns). The push or pull that moves the lever is called the **force,** or **effort.** The next activity will help you see how a lever works.

2. What is the hinge, or turning point, of a lever called?

All these machines are levers. Put your finger on the fulcrum of each one.

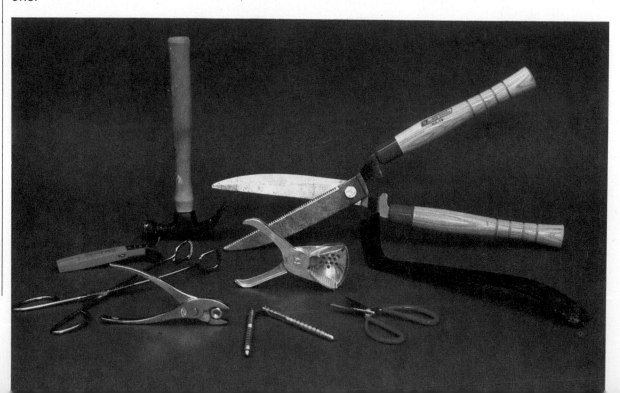

Activity 31

How does a lever help do work?

You need:

Empty shoebox
Sand
Books (all the same size)
Board (1 m long)
Metric ruler

Sandpaper
Masking tape
Large juice can
   (unopened)

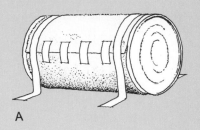

A

A. Tape the sandpaper to the outside of the can. Put the can on its side on the floor. Run pieces of masking tape over the can. Stick the ends of the tape to the floor.

B. Place the board over the can. Make sure the middle of the board is on the can.

C. Fill the shoebox with sand. Put it on one end of the board. Start piling books on the other end of the board. Keep doing this until the box of sand is balanced.

D. Do the activity again. This time, pile the books about 30 cm away from the end of the board.

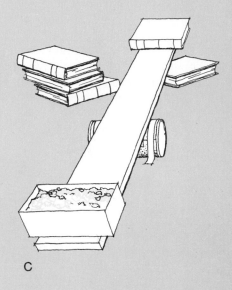

C

Answer these:

1. How many books did it take to balance the box of sand?

2. How many books did it take to balance the sand when you put the books 30 cm from the end?

3. Why were you told to put sandpaper on the can?

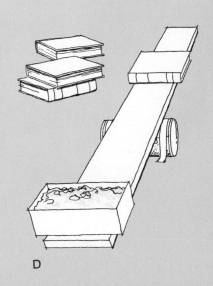

D

Perhaps you never thought of a road as being a "machine." But sometimes it is. This twisting mountain road is a screw. Find a sentence on this page that explains why.

THREE MORE MACHINES

Another simple machine is the **inclined** (in klīnd′) **plane.** An inclined plane is any ramp, or slope. It is always higher on one end then on the other. Have you ever walked up a ramp, or slope? It was easier than climbing straight up a ladder. Roads going up a mountain often wind back and forth. This makes it easier for a car to climb the hill. A road like that is made up of many inclined planes.

The **wedge** (wej) is still another simple machine. A wedge is made up of two inclined planes. The inclined planes come together to form a sharp edge. Many cutting tools are sharpened wedges. The bow, or front, of a boat is a wedge. How does a boat's bow make work easier?

The **screw** is also a simple machine. A screw is an inclined plane that is twisted into a spiral. Look at a bolt or screw. Trace the screw's thread with a pencil or with your finger. How is the screw like a wedge?

Activity 32 will help you learn more about inclined planes and doing work.

Activity 32

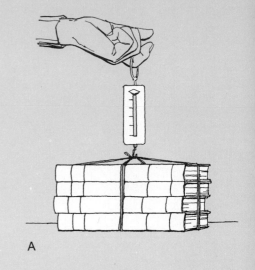

A

How does an inclined plane make work easier?

You need:

8 books
String
Spring scale
Board (about 1.5 m long)

A. Tie 4 books together. Weigh them with a spring scale. Record their weight.

B. Place the other 4 books under one end of the board to form a ramp.

C. Pull the books up the board. Make sure the spring scale is hooked to the string.

D. Read the scale to find out how much force is needed to pull the books.

Answer these:

1. How much did the books weigh when you first used the spring scale?

2. How much force did it take to pull the books up the board?

3. Was the force more or less than the weight of the books?

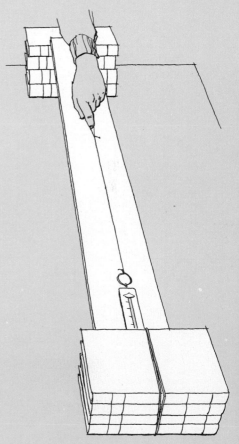

C

THE LAST TWO

The **pulley** is another simple machine. A pulley is a wheel with a rope or belt moving over it. Force is put on one end of the rope. The object to be moved is on the other end. As the rope or belt moves, the wheel turns. The rim of the wheel is often grooved. This keeps the rope or belt from slipping. Pulleys that are fastened in one place are called fixed pulleys. The pulley at the top of a flagpole is a fixed pulley. Pulleys that are not fastened are called movable pulleys.

This picture was taken on a farm in the state of Washington. It shows a wheel-and-axle. You can easily see how this kind of machine got its name.

A **wheel-and-axle** is just what the name says. It is a machine made of a wheel that turns on a center post, or axle. You can see many of these around you. Think of a car or your school bus. Where are the wheels-and-axles? You probably named the four wheels on the car or bus.

But don't forget the steering wheel. Its axle is the steering column. Think how hard it would be to steer a car without the steering wheel.

Earlier you learned that a pencil sharpener is made of simple machines. There are at least two different kinds of simple machines in most pencil sharpeners. With your teacher's help, look carefully at your pencil sharpener. What simple machines can you see?

COMPLEX MACHINES

Are you surprised that there are only six simple machines? When most people talk about machines, they do not mean simple machines. They usually are talking about **complex** (kəm pleks') **machines.** A complex machine is made up of two or more simple machines.

Have someone bring a two-wheeled bicycle to school. Turn it upside down. Make sure it rests on its handlebars and seat. Turn the pedals slowly. What simple machines do you see?

There are thousands of kinds of complex machines. Each of these machines is made up of many parts. Each part is a simple machine. Watch some complex machines at work. Look for the simple machines. There are two or more of them in each complex machine.

This large crane and electromagnet is a complex machine. See how many simple machines you can find in the picture. These old cars will be used in making more steel. This is important recycling of resources.

2

Machines and Work

As you learned earlier, in order to do work something must be moved. You also learned that work can be measured. To measure work done, you must know how far an object is moved. You must also know how much force was used. The force is the push, pull, or lift on an object. To measure work done, force is multiplied by distance. This is so important that we'll repeat it. The force used times the distance moved equals the work done.

The distance is always measured in meters. The force is always measured in newtons. A **newton** is a unit of force in the metric system. The work done will then be measured in newton meters. Scientists have another word for a newton meter. It is a **joule** (jül). A joule is named

Much work is being done at this lumber mill. How could you measure how much?

after the English scientist James P. Joule. In the upper grades you will learn more about measuring work. For now, just remember that work is measured by multiplying two things. These are the distance an object moves multiplied by the force needed to move it.

Look at the pictures on this page. In which one is no work being done? In which one is work being done?

Which of these children is doing work? How can you tell?

WORK AND ENERGY

Every day you do work. You are always pushing, pulling, or lifting something. Machines also do work when they push, pull, or lift something. What do people and machines use when they do work? They use force. But there would be no force if there were no energy. It does not matter whether the work is hard or easy. No person or machine can do work without using energy. That is an important fact of science.

There are several kinds of energy. Two of the ones that you know are heat and light. But mechanical energy, the energy of motion, and electrical energy are other forms. There are three others that you might not know so well. They are sound energy, chemical energy, and nuclear energy. To do work, a machine must use one of those kinds of energy. Of course some machines may use many different kinds of energy. All the objects shown at the right are machines. Decide what kind of energy makes each one run.

Many machines change energy from one form to another. Think about these machines: toaster, radio, electric mixer, and television set. What kinds of energy go into those machines? What kinds come out?

Anything that changes energy from one form to another is a machine. These are machines found in many kitchens.

3. What is another name for energy of motion?

Where is chemical energy being used in this picture? Don't forget the girls' bodies.

Now think about your own body. You too require energy. Where does the energy for your body come from? It comes from the chemical energy in the food you eat. When this chemical energy is used, some of it changes to heat energy. This keeps you warm. Some changes into mechanical energy to move the parts of your body. You are using mechanical energy when you ride a bike. Is mechan-

ical energy used to pound a nail with a hammer? to open a can of juice with a can opener? Where does the energy you need to do these things come from?

There is another place chemical energy is used in machines. Chemical energy is changed to electrical energy in dry cells. The batteries in flashlights are dry cells. You may have used a flashlight outside at night. Or you may have toys that run on flashlight batteries. What energy changes take place in the toys shown on page 164?

What about your school bus or family car? Where does its energy come from? You know it comes from the gasoline. There is chemical energy in the gasoline. When it is used, the chemical energy changes to moving, or mechanical, energy. It also changes to other kinds of energy. Can you name one?

FRICTION AND MACHINES

Rub some sandpaper on a block of wood. Did you notice how warm the sandpaper got? Whenever two objects rub against one another, there is **friction** (frik′ shən). The energy used to overcome friction makes objects warm. Friction also makes it harder to do work. In Activity 33 you will see how friction makes work harder.

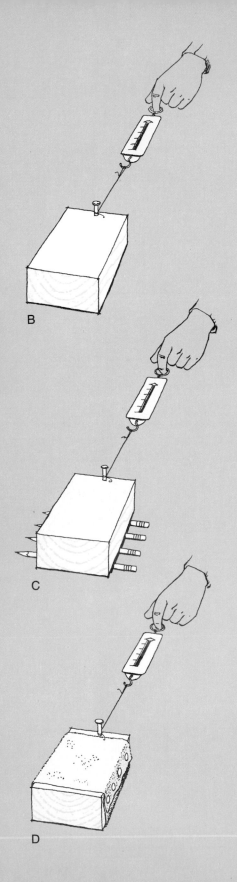

Activity 33

How does friction make work harder?

You need:

A piece of scrap lumber	String
Sandpaper	4 round pencils
Nail	4 thumbtacks
Hammer	Spring scale

A. Drive a nail partway into one end of the wood. Make a loop in one end of the string. Slip the loop over the hook on the scale. Tie the other end of the string to the nail.

B. Use the scale to pull the wood slowly over the floor. Keep a record of how much force was needed.

C. Place the board on the 4 round pencils. Slowly pull the board over the floor. Keep a record of how much force was needed.

D. Wrap the sandpaper around the board. Tack it to the board as shown. Pull the board slowly over the floor.

Answer these:

1. How much force was needed in step **B?** in step **C?** in step **D?**
2. In which step was there the most friction? In which step was there the least?
3. How did friction make it harder to pull the board across the floor?

Suppose you wanted to slide a heavy box across a floor. Would it be easier if the floor were rough or smooth? There would be friction in both cases. But there would be less friction if the floor were smooth.

How can you cut down friction in a machine? One way is to smooth the surfaces of the parts. You can make some surfaces smooth with oil or grease. The surfaces then slide on a thin coating of oil or grease. This is called **lubrication** (lü brə kā′ shən). Why is lubrication important?

Another way to cut down friction is to stop the amount of rubbing. Think about sliding the heavy box across a floor. Suppose the bottom of the box is 1 meter by 1 meter. You would have that much wood rubbing against the same amount of floor. But now suppose you put wagon wheels on the box. The wheels would roll instead of rub. Activity 34 will help you observe this way of reducing friction.

So far we have only talked about harmful friction. But sometimes friction is useful. Why do you wear gym shoes in gym class? Have you ever played in the gym in your stocking feet? What does this show about friction?

The mechanic is greasing a car. How does this cut down on friction?

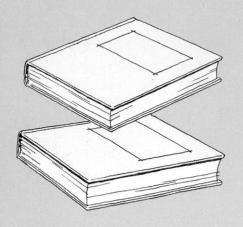

Activity 34

How are rollers like wheels?

You need:
Metric ruler
2 pieces of cord (each piece 1 m long)
2 books (each the same size)
11 round pencils (all the same length)

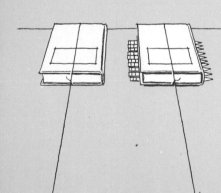

A. Tie a piece of cord around each book. Tie the loose end of each cord to the ruler. Make sure the cords are the same length.

B. Put the 11 pencils under one book. Rest the other book on the desk.

C. Hold the middle of the ruler with your thumb and first finger. Pull the books slowly forward.

Answer these:
1. Which book moved more easily?
2. Why did one book move more easily than the other one?
3. What happened to the ends of the ruler as you pulled? Why?
4. Why did the books act as they did?
5. How did the pencils reduce friction?

SAFETY AND MACHINES

You know how common automobile accidents are. But do you know where most accidents happen? They occur at home. Many home accidents are caused by careless use of tools. Tools are machines. All machines, big and small, must be used carefully.

You must think when you use machines. You should know what you are doing. And you must also think about your safety. Belts and gears on machines should be covered. If your clothes flop around, they may catch on machines. Sometimes machines throw off small pieces of matter. That is why you should protect all parts of your body. Protect your eyes with safety glasses. Remember, machines help you work only if you use them safely.

You must remember to think about the machine. Use machines only for the jobs they are made for. Also, keep them in good working order. A damaged machine is dangerous. It also wastes energy.

Most schools have rules about wearing safety glasses. This girl is working with a machine in shop class. Her eyes are protected from flying bits of wood the machine may throw off. She also wears glasses like these in her chemistry class. Safety in the classroom is a serious matter. It should not be taken lightly.

Checking What You Learned

USING SCIENCE WORDS

You learned some important new science words in this unit. Write the numbers 1 – 6 on a sheet of paper. Then read the sentences below. After each number, write the word or words that correctly complete the sentence. Use these words: <u>complex machine</u>, <u>energy</u>, <u>force</u>, <u>friction</u>, <u>fulcrum</u>, <u>inclined plane</u>, <u>lever</u>, <u>lubrication</u>, <u>pulley</u>, <u>resistance</u>, <u>screw</u>, <u>simple machine</u>, <u>wedge</u>, <u>wheel-and-axle</u>, <u>work</u>.

1. To measure _____, multiply the distance something moves by the force needed to move it.
2. A wheel with a rope or line moving over it is a _____.
3. No machine can work without a supply of _____.
4. A machine made up of several different simple machines is called a _____.
5. Machines are often oiled or greased to reduce _____.
6. The hinge, or turning point, of a lever is called the _____.

CHECKING THE FACTS

1. Column A lists some types of work. The six types of simple machines are listed in column B. Write the letters **a – e** on a sheet of paper. Decide which type of machine would be best for each job. Write your choice beside each letter on your paper.

A	B
a. Steering a car	pulley
b. Raising a flag	wedge
	inclined plane
c. Moving a heavy box onto a truck	screw
	lever
d. Opening a can of tomato juice	wheel-and-axle
e. Prying open a can of paint	

ACTIVITIES TO TRY

1. Make some small pulleys out of spools and string. Make a sign that tells how a pulley works. Draw or cut out magazine pictures that show different ways pulleys are used. Put these pictures on the classroom bulletin board.

2. There may be a new house or building being built near your school. If so, plan a trip to the building. Be sure you have permission from the workers. Stay out of the workers' way. But notice how many different kinds of machines they are using. Decide what kinds of energy are used to run the machines. Draw a mural for your classroom that shows the building.

IDEAS TO THINK ABOUT

1. Look for a picture of a pyramid. Pyramids were built before people had complex machines. What kinds of machines might have been used to build the pyramids? How long do you think it took to build one pyramid?

2. Sometimes friction is useful. Sometimes it is harmful. List three ways in which friction can be useful. Also list three ways by which friction can be reduced.

SCIENCE AND YOU

Machines are used by everyone. Some day you may be a mechanic who repairs cars. You will use tools made by a machinist or a tool-and-die maker. Watchmakers use some of the same tools mechanics use. Homemakers and office workers use both simple and complex machines. Even people in sports use machines. A baseball player uses a bat; a tennis player uses a racket. Why are bats and rackets called machines?

Living Communities

Plants and animals live almost everywhere in the world. They live in jungles, deserts, oceans, and snow-covered lands. Some live in your backyard.

There are many different kinds of plants and animals in the world. Usually, many different kinds live together in one place. The plants and animals living in a place form a **community** (kə myü′ nə tē). It is a community of living things.

The plants and animals in one community may be different from those in other communities. You would not find elephants in the community in your backyard. But you might find ants and dandelions there. You would not look for banana trees in Alaska. But you might find polar bears there.

When it rains, a desert blooms.

1

Food and Life

The word <u>community</u> usually means the place where people live. Your town or city is a community. Every town or city must have certain things for its people. It must have a supply of food and water. A community must also have houses or homes for people to live in. Houses or other buildings give protection to people.

Plants and animals need the same things in their communities. Plants and animals must have energy. Green plants get the energy they need from sunlight. They use the energy of sunlight to make food. Animals and nongreen plants cannot make their own food. They must get their energy from other living or once-living things.

This is a community in Delaware. Like other communities, it has homes and churches. There are also stores, schools, and gas stations. What else do you see?

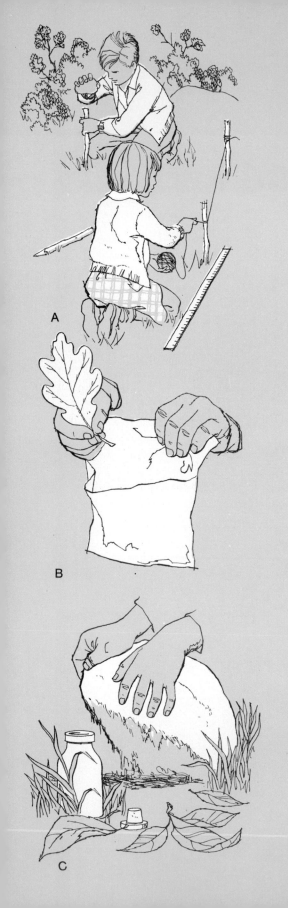

Activity 35

What living things can you find in a small community?

You need:

Plastic sandwich bags
Empty pill bottles with caps
Meterstick or metric ruler
Trowel
Notebook

A. You will need to choose a helper for this activity. Go together to a park or vacant lot near your school. Mark off a section of the park or lot. Make the section one meter square. The square can be marked with pebbles or sticks. The marked square is the "community" you will explore.

B. If local laws permit, collect samples of the living things in the community. Put any plants you collect in plastic bags. Collect only one of each kind of plant. If you have a tree or bush, take only one leaf.

If plants cannot be collected, make drawings of the plants you find.

C. Look for animal life in the community. Look below the surface. You can dig with your trowel. Put in bottles any animals you find. Record where you find the animals.

Answer these:

1. What did the community look like?
2. What kinds of plants did you find?
3. What kinds of animals did you find?

Some animals eat plants for food. Some animals eat other animals. Most non-green plants get their energy from the bodies of dead plants or animals.

Some animals use large amounts of energy. A hummingbird eats nearly twice its weight in food each day. It uses much energy because it moves very fast. Suppose you ate that much food every day. How many kilograms of food would you eat?

Plants and animals must have water to live. Some plants and animals can live only in water. Plants that live on land must get water from the air or soil. Most animals that live on land get water by drinking it. There are some places in deserts where there is no water to drink. Animals living in these places must get their water in another way. They get it from the food they eat. Some kinds of rats and mice get their water that way.

Plants and animals need protection. Some plants need protection from animals. Many plants are killed if their tops are eaten by animals. Other kinds of plants, such as grasses, are not. They simply grow new tops from their parts underground.

Most animals have shelters in which they live. Some birds build nests in the shelter of branches and leaves of trees. Others build nests in the shelter of weeds

This animal gets its energy from grass. The grass stores energy from the sun.

These are one type of gopher. They are called "prairie dogs." They have this name because they make a barking sound like that of a dog. They live in burrows.

and grass. Pheasants, quail, and grouse are such birds. These birds cannot live where there is no grass or weeds.

Some animals live in holes or tunnels in the ground. A tunnel dug by an animal is called a **burrow** (bėr′ ō). Foxes, coyotes, moles, and gophers live in burrows. Animals that live underground are protected from most other animals. The temperatures of deep soil do not change much. They do not change nearly as much as air temperatures. Animals that live underground are protected from heat and cold. Why do few animals live underground in swamps and riverbanks?

Activity 36

How do underground temperatures compare with air temperatures?

You need:

2 Celsius thermometers
Metric ruler
Clock or watch
Notebook
Trowel

A. Try to do this step before 10:00 A.M. Push a trowel about 5 cm into the soil. Make the hole just large enough to hold a thermometer.

B. Put one thermometer into the soil. Put the other thermometer on top of the ground. Wait 5 minutes. Then measure and record the temperature in each place.

C. Do this step in the afternoon. Measure the temperature in the two places again. Find out how much the temperature has changed in each place.

A

Answer these:

1. Where was it warmer in the morning?
2. Where was it warmer in the afternoon?
3. What was the difference between the morning and afternoon temperatures of the air?
4. What was the difference between the morning and afternoon temperatures underground?

B

This lioness is waiting to attack a herd of animals. What may the herd eat? What does a lion pack eat?

HERDS, PACKS, AND COLONIES

Some animals live in large groups. These groups of animals have special names. Groups of animals that eat mostly plants are called **herds** (hėrdz). Groups of hunting animals are often called **packs.** Groups of animals that share the work of living form **colonies** (kol'ə nēz). Most animals that live in colonies get their food from plants.

Cattle, sheep, elephants, and reindeer live in herds. Cattle and sheep eat grass. Elephants eat many kinds of plants. They eat grass, small bushes, and banana trees. Reindeer live where there are green plants only part of the year. Most of the year, reindeer must dig under snow to find food. All these animals are called **herbivores** (hėr′ bə vôrz). Herbivores are animals that eat only plants. Name some other herbivores that live in herds.

Herbivores eat large numbers of plants each day. They are eating almost every minute they are not sleeping. Most plant material contains small amounts of energy that can be used by animals. So, herbivores must eat many plants to stay alive.

Wolves, coyotes, and hyenas live in packs. All these animals are meat eaters. Animals that eat only other animals are called **carnivores** (kär′ nə vôrz). What pets are carnivores?

This coyote lives in Yellowstone Park. It is a carnivore.

Carnivores do not eat as frequently as plant eaters do. There is much energy in meat. There is more energy in meat than in most plant material.

Carnivores that live in packs hunt for food in groups. This helps them catch and kill animals. Working together, they can kill animals larger than themselves.

Animals that live in colonies help each other. The members do different jobs.

As many as twelve beavers may live in a colony. The members of the colony build a dam across a stream. The dam forms a pond. Their home, or lodge, is built in the pond.

Different members of the beaver colony do different kinds of work. Some collect tree branches and twigs for food. Others cut down nearby trees with their teeth. Some work on the dam and lodge. They repair damage caused by washouts. Are beavers herbivores or carnivores?

You can see a beaver lodge in the bottom left corner of this picture. Why is a beaver lodge something like a beehive?

Penguins (pen′gwinz) are birds that live in colonies. There may be thousands of penguins in one colony. They lay eggs in nests. Both males and females keep the eggs warm. Both help raise the young birds.

After the young penguins hatch, they gather together. One adult penguin usually watches them. The other adults may be out searching for food. They eat fish and other animals from the ocean. A few weeks after hatching, penguins can find their own food.

Many insects live in colonies. These insects are called **social** (sō′ shəl) **insects.** Honeybees are the best-known social insects.

About 60 000 bees live in the average bee colony. Most of the bees in the colony are worker bees. Worker bees do many jobs. The workers may act as guards or nurses. Others act as housekeepers. Most workers are busy collecting food. The queen bee has only one job. She lays eggs. All young bees in a colony hatch from eggs laid by the queen.

Bees use **nectar** (nek′tər) and **pollen** (pol′ ən) from flowers for food. Nectar is carried into the hive and stored as honey. Pollen is also stored in the hive. Honey supplies bees with energy. Pollen supplies them with proteins, vitamins, and minerals.

This beekeeper is moving a swarm of bees into a beehive. Bees in the hive store more honey than they will eat. This extra honey may be used as food by people.

These ants are taking care of pupae in a colony. The pupae will hatch into new ants.

Perhaps you have seen some of the beautiful large nests of hornets. These are great big balls that seem to be made of paper. They can be found hanging from high branches in the woods. These nests should never be disturbed! Hornets are social insects too. Other social insects that you may know are wasps and ants.

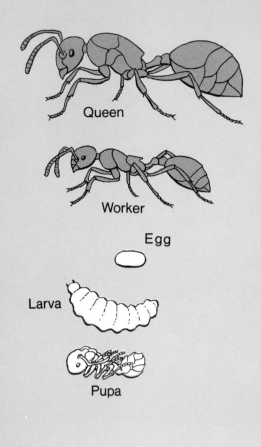

Queen

Worker

Egg

Larva

Pupa

Activity 37

Do ants share the work of a colony?

You need:

Ant cage (with sandy soil)	Shovel
	Black paper
Pieces of cardboard	Metric ruler
Food (lunch scraps)	Water
Medicine dropper	
Collecting bottles	

A. Several people must work together on this step. Find an ant colony outdoors. One person will dig for the ants. Others should be ready to pick up ants. Also pick up eggs, larvae, and pupae. Eggs look like grains of wheat or rice. Larvae look like short, white worms. Pupae look like baby ants in a shell-like skin. Everyone should look for the queen ant. The queen will be larger than the other ants. Everything should be picked up with pieces of cardboard.

Dig from 15 to 20 cm deep. The queen will probably be near the bottom of the colony. Collect at least 50 worker ants. Drop collected ants into collecting bottles. Collect all the larvae and pupae you see.

B. Put the collected ants into the ant cage. Cover the sides with black paper.

A

C. Put different bits of food into two or three bottle caps. The food should be broken into tiny pieces. Put the filled caps on the soil in the cage.

Fill the medicine dropper with water. Put the water on the soil. This must be done every other day.

D. Observe the ants once each day for 2 weeks. Do this by lifting the black paper covering the sides. See if you can learn enough about ants to answer these questions.

Answer these:

1. How long did it take for the ants to build a nest?

2. What did worker ants do with the eggs and pupae?

3. What does an ant nest look like?

4. Do ants do a lot of traveling underground?

5. Why must workers feed the queen?

6. What kinds of jobs did you see worker ants doing?

7. Can ants recognize other ants that do not belong to their colony?

Groups of Living Things

You learned that every living thing must have energy. Different living things in a community may have different sources of energy. The source of energy for green plants is sunlight. Green plants use the energy of sunlight to make food. They use food to grow. Some food made by green plants is stored. Food may be stored in roots, stems, or leaves. The energy of food is then in the parts of plants. Heat is one kind of energy. You can get a lot of energy from burning leaves and stems of plants. Where does this energy come from?

Many nongreen plants get their energy from green plants that have died. Worms and many other small animals also use dead plants for food. They do not kill the plants. They simply use the dead plants as a source of food.

This horse is eating "stored sunlight."

Some living things help others get energy. Have you seen a vine climbing a tree? Poison ivy and wild grapes can grow on tree trunks. These vines might not get enough light if they grew under trees. They get more light by growing higher. Trees help vines get energy.

Many animals help other animals get food. Small fish often swim near sharks. Sharks kill large fish for food. Small fish eat pieces of those fish. How might squirrels help birds get seeds and nuts?

Many plants and animals use the same sources of energy. They compete with each other for energy. Plants sometimes compete for light. They do this by the way they grow. One plant may grow faster than other plants. The leaves of this plant get light. Plants that grow more slowly will be in shade. They will not get as much light. They may not get enough light to live.

Some light passes between the leaves of trees. Grass and other plants grow under such trees as oaks, maples, and birches. But they must be plants that can live with some shade. Why do few plants live under pine and spruce trees?

Animals may also compete for energy. Field mice and quail eat many of the same foods. Mice have a good sense of smell. They can find seeds by smelling them. Quail find seeds by seeing them.

1. Do fast-growing plants usually grow in the sun or in shade?

They use claws and beaks to uncover seeds. A good sense of smell helps mice compete with quail. What helps quail compete with mice?

Any living thing may be food for another living thing. Some plants and animals are protected from being eaten. Some plants have a juice that tastes bitter. Most animals will not eat those plants. Many other plants are protected by stickers or thorns. Name some plants that are protected in this way.

Do you think this thistle is used as food by animals? Why?

When the hognose snake is in danger, it "plays dead." How does this protect the snake?

Animals protect themselves in many different ways. The opossum (ə pos′əm) and the hognose snake both hiss and strike at attackers. But then they may suddenly "play dead." The opossum rolls over on its back. Its mouth falls open. Its eyes roll back in its head.

The hognose snake also rolls over on its back. It goes limp. If you turn it right side up, it turns over again. The animals act this way when they are in danger.

Some birds have a special way of protecting their nests. When something nears the nest, the mother bird acts crippled. She may drag one wing and flutter along the ground. She stays just out of

reach of the attacker. This often leads the attacker away from the nest. Killdeers and pheasants are birds that do this.

A hedgehog rolls itself into a ball when it is in danger. Its back is covered with spines. Its head and toes are pulled under its body. Not even a hungry animal will bite this spiny ball.

Some animals are hard to see. This is also a kind of protection. It is called **protective coloration** (prə tek′ tiv kul ə rā′ shən). For example, deer have colors much like those of dry leaves. Deer are hard to see if they do not move. Young deer have no odor. Meat eaters cannot find them by smell.

The piping plover is a bird that "pretends" to have a broken wing.

When there is danger, a hedgehog rolls itself into a ball.

Can you find the owl in this picture? This is a good example of protective coloration.

All the following animals have defenses. What defenses does each have? (Here are some hints: Some have sharp teeth. Others can climb well. Some have hard body coverings.)

Skunk	Porcupine	Turtle
Robin	Weasel	Fox
Toad	Bear	Snake
Rabbit	Wasp	Deer

Activity 38

How many birds can you see?

Study the picture. There are **ptarmigans** (tär′ mə gəns) among the rocks. Count the ptarmigans in the picture.

Answer these:

1. How many ptarmigans did you find?
2. Ptarmigans are eaten by foxes. But a fox must see a ptarmigan to catch it. Some birds move when danger is near. Other birds "freeze." This means they do not move. What do you think a ptarmigan does?

All living things need water. These animals are drinking from a watering place in South Africa.

COMPETING FOR RESOURCES

Plants and animals do not always compete for things they need. All plants and animals must have air. But they do not compete for air. There is enough air for all living things.

Most communities do not have enough of everything for all plants and animals. In deserts there is not enough water for all living things. Plants that grow there must compete for water. Some desert plants have many long roots. They get more water than plants with few roots. Think about plants that grow in water or in swamps. Would they be more likely to have large or small roots?

Animals also compete for water in dry places. Desert animals often drink from small puddles and pools. Camels usually live in deserts. A camel can drink about 60 **liters** (lē′ tərz) of water at one time. This water will last from 6 to 10 days. Suppose a camel drank from a very small pool. The pool held only 40 liters of water. How would this affect other animals near the pool? Think about the animals that live near you. Can they live without water as long as a camel can?

Animals sometimes compete for places to live. Have you seen one bird chase another from a yard? The bird doing the chasing is keeping others from its home. Many birds keep other birds from the area near their nests. This area is called the bird's **territory** (ter′ə tôr ē). Many birdsongs are warnings to other birds. The songs are warnings not to invade the territory.

2. Some animals have an area they mark off for their own home. What is this called?

This yellow-shafted flicker has found a home. It is a hole in a hollow tree.

Birds that live in birdhouses once lived in hollow trees. Long ago there were more hollow trees than there are today. People have cut down many forests. Few dead trees are allowed to stand. Birds often compete for holes in trees. They also compete for birdhouses. Why are birdhouses made with holes of certain sizes?

Activity 39

Do animals of the same kind compete with each other?

You need:

Aquarium with guppies
Tropical fish food (granular or flake)
1 piece of lean hamburger (smaller than the head of a match)

A. Feed the fish in your aquarium with regular fish food. Put in at least two small pieces of food for each fish. Watch the fish as they eat. Find out if all the fish start eating at the same time. Try to find out if each fish gets some food. Look for signs that the fish are competing for the food.

Wait until tomorrow to do the next step.

B. Put one small piece of lean meat into the aquarium. Watch the fish as they eat. Look for signs that the fish are competing for the food.

Answer these:

1. Are all the fish the same size?
2. Did all the fish get some food?
3. For which food did the fish compete more?
4. How do fish compete for food?
5. Which fish got the most meat?
6. Wild guppies live in rivers in South America. Suppose there was not enough food for all guppies in a river. Which guppies would get the most food?

In 1926 this lake was used as a source of water power for a flour mill. It was also used for fishing and swimming.

CHANGES IN A COMMUNITY

Look at the lake in the picture above. It was once a favorite spot for many people. The water was fresh and clean. People used the lake for swimming, fishing, and boating. Plants grew in the clear water. The lake was the home of fish, water insects, and turtles.

Water in the lake came from streams. These streams started far away, in hills. For a long time the streams were fresh and clean. Then farmers began cutting trees on the hillsides. They cleared the land and planted crops. Rainstorms washed soil from the fields into the

streams. The water became very muddy. The muddy water flowed to the lake. The mud settled to the bottom of the lake. The lake became shallow.

The living community in the lake changed. Many fish and water plants could not live in muddy water. Plants and animals living near the lake also changed.

Swampy land formed where there was once water. New kinds of plants and animals formed a new community. What kinds of plants and animals might be living in this community?

Turn the page. See what the lake looks like today.

By 1946, twenty years later, the lake had filled with silt. The lake had become a swamp, with a small creek wandering through it.

TRY THIS

Not all communities are large. A community may be found under paper and cardboard litter. A community may be found in the shade of a trash can. A wet community may form under a leaking faucet. Explore the areas near your home and school. Find at least one such community that has changed. Look for one that has changed because of something humans have done. Keep a record of what you find.

Today this same area is good farm-
land. The soil is good for growing
many crops. Where did the rich soil
come from?

LIFE AND DEATH

Look at the picture of a fence. The fence belongs to a farmer who likes wild-life. Many wild flowers grow along the fence. Grasshoppers and other insects live on the plants. They eat the plants. Field mice and birds live among the plants. Both mice and birds eat the seeds of the plants. The birds also eat many of the insects. Sometimes a fox hunts along the fence. The fox may catch an animal that lives among the plants. Foxes eat mostly mice.

New life is always starting in the community along the fence. New plants grow from seeds. Thousands of insects hatch from eggs. Mice are born in grass-lined nests. Birds are hatched in nests. This

A fence community in Colorado. Many kinds of plants and animals live here.

small community has many thousands of living things.

You might think the community would get more and more crowded. But it does not. The number of plants and animals stays about the same. Plants and animals are always dying. Some plants die because they are eaten by insects. Some insects die because they are eaten by birds. Foxes kill birds and mice. Some plants and animals die when they become old.

Why do some plants and animals live and others die? You have learned that plants compete with each other as they grow. There is not enough space for all the plants that grow from seeds. Which of the new plants will most likely live?

Insects do not usually eat all of a plant. Some insects only suck juices from plants. Other insects eat parts of stems and leaves. Some plants can quickly grow new stems and leaves. Other plants cannot grow new parts. Which plants will be more likely to live? Why do insects not eat some kinds of plants?

Not all insects will be eaten by birds. How might some insects avoid being eaten? Which of the insects will most likely be caught and eaten? Which mice and birds will escape from a hunting fox?

The greatest danger to all life along the fence is people. Dead grass along the fence will burn. A careless person might start a fire. Almost all life in the community could be killed by fire.

Many farmers use chemical sprays to kill weeds. Suppose the farmer sprayed the plants along the fence. Grass plants might not be killed by the spray. But most wild flowers would be killed. Fewer seeds would be grown in the community.

Killing plants with spray will affect animals in the community. There will be less food for insects. Only insects that eat grass will live. There will be fewer seeds and insects for birds to eat. The birds will move to a new place to live.

Mice will also move from along the fence. They may move into the farmer's barn. They may eat the stored grain. The farmer will then try to kill the mice. The farmer may use poisoned grain to kill the mice. Many mice will eat the poison and die. Some mice will smell or taste the poison. They may not eat enough to kill them. These mice will live and continue to eat the farmer's crops.

Foxes will not find as many wild things to eat. Some hungry fox may eat the farmer's chickens. Other foxes may be afraid of humans. They may not come near the farmer's chickens. Which foxes will be more likely to live? Why may killing weeds cause many problems for farmers?

Activity 40

Could an insect that eats some plants be helping other plants grow?

You need:

Tomato seeds	Scissors
2 plastic pots	2 small aluminum pans
Vermiculite	water

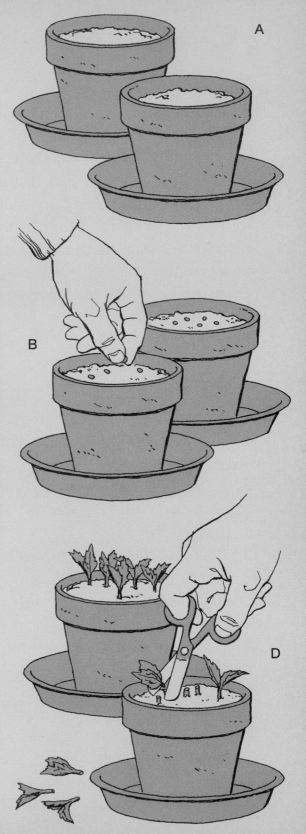

A. Nearly fill the 2 pots with vermiculite. Put each pot in a pan. Pour water on the vermiculite until it runs from the pot.

B. Plant 5 tomato seeds near the middle of each pot. Add just enough dry vermiculite to cover the seeds.

C. Put the pots in a warm, light place. Wait until the plants have leaves before you do the next step.

D. You are going to act like a plant-eating insect. In one pot, cut off the tops of all plants but one. Do not cut any plants in the other pot. Put equal amounts of water into each pot when they need water. If the plants are fertilized, use equal amounts in each pot.

E. Watch the plants grow for 3 weeks. Compare the plants in the two pots.

Answer these:

1. Which pot has the largest plant?
2. Why might a plant grow better if an insect eats other plants nearby?

Checking What You Learned

USING SCIENCE WORDS

Some of the important science words you learned in this unit are listed below. They are in column B. Write the numbers 1−5 on a sheet of paper. Then read the phrases in column A. Decide which term in column B best matches each phrase in column A. Write the correct term next to each number on your paper. (You need not use all the terms listed in column B.)

A	B
1. Animals that eat only other animals	burrow
	carnivores
2. A tunnel in the ground where animals live	colony
	community
3. Insects that live in colonies and divide their work	herbivores
	pack
	protective
4. Animals that feed only on plants	coloration
	social
5. The coloring of some animals that makes them hard to see	insects
	territory

CHECKING THE FACTS

Write the numbers 1−6 on a sheet of paper. Then read the sentences below. Decide whether each one is true, or false. If it is true, write <u>T</u> next to the number. If it is false, write <u>F</u>.

1. All the plants and animals that live in one place form a community.
2. Animals need energy, but plants do not.
3. Carnivores are plant eaters. They eat much more food than herbivores do.
4. Groups of hunting animals are called herds.
5. Social insects live in packs in burrows in the ground.
6. Farmers who use chemical weed killers can destroy communities of living things.

ACTIVITIES TO TRY

1. Perhaps there is a small pond or stream near your home or school. If there is, plan a trip to it. Look along the edge of the water. Collect any living things you find. Put pond water in the jars. Carry them back to school. Watch the plants and animals for several minutes. Draw pictures of them. Find out what they are and why they live in a pond.

2. Try to find some pictures of places around your town before buildings were there. Perhaps you can find a picture of the land your school is on. Or you might find a picture of land where there is now a shopping center. Think about the kinds of living things that lived there before the buildings went up. What may have happened to those living things?

IDEAS TO THINK ABOUT

1. Some animals are hard to see in their environments. Those animals have body colors like the plants around them. Think about the animals listed below. How does their color help protect them?

Tree frog   Rabbit
Pheasant   Walking stick
Deer   Polar bear
Zebra   Snowy owl

2. Some animals are pests to people. What animals may be pests to a farmer? What are some animals that are pests to you? How are these pests alike? How are they different?

SCIENCE AND YOU

Did you ever wonder who takes care of the animals in a zoo? Zookeepers and veterinarians do. But wild animals also need protection. Conservation officers and park rangers protect wild animals. Beekeepers and fishing guides must also protect living communities.

GLOSSARY

Some words in this book may be new to you. They may be hard for you to say. Some of these words are science words. Science words are shown in bold print like this: **atmosphere.** Hard-to-say-words are spelled in two different ways in the book. This is done the first time the word is used. The second spelling tells you how to say the word. It shows the sounds certain letters or groups of letters have. Use this key to learn those sounds.

Key to Pronunciation

a	hat, cap	i	it, pin	sh	she, rush	ə	represents:
ā	age, face	ī	ice, five	th	thin, both		a in about
ã	care, air	ng	long, bring	ᴛʜ	then, smooth		e in taken
ä	father, far	o	hot, rock	u	cup, butter		i in pencil
ch	child, much	ō	open, go	u̇	full, put		o in lemon
e	let, best	ô	order, all	ü	rule, move		u in circus
ē	equal, see	oi	oil, voice	zh	measure, seizure		
ėr	term, learn	ou	house, out				

The Key to Pronunciation above is from *The World Book Dictionary* copyright © 1970, by Doubleday & Company, Inc. Reprinted by permission of the publisher.

atmosphere   A layer of gases surrounding a planet. (p. 17)

atoms   Basic units of matter. (p. 142)

bacteria   Small living things that can cause disease. (p. 109)

boulders   Big rocks. Some are as large as a room. (p. 55)

burrow   A tunnel dug by an animal. (p. 178)

calcite   A mineral found in limestone and some other rocks. (p. 56)

Calories   Units used to measure the amount of energy in food. (p. 103)

carbon dioxide   One of the gases that make up the atmosphere. (p. 57)

carnivores   Animals that eat only other animals. (p. 182)

change of state   The change of a solid, liquid, or gas to another form. (p. 138)

chemical change   Change in the chemical composition of matter. (p. 144)

clay   Closely packed soil that can hold much water. (p. 60)

coleus   A type of green plant. (p. 84)

colonies   Groups of living things of the same kind that live together as a community. (p. 180)

comets Objects that travel in a path through the solar system. They have a head and a long tail. (p. 20)

community Groups of different plants and animals that live together. (p. 173)

complex machines Machines made up of two or more simple machines. (p. 159)

contour plowing Plowing across hills instead of up and down. This helps stop the washing away of topsoil. (p. 65)

core The inside layer of the earth below the mantle. (p. 42)

craters Large, often deep holes in the earth's surface. (p. 23)

crust The outer layer of the earth. (p. 41)

diet The food a person eats. (p. 114)

dunes Hills of sand piled up by the wind. (p. 50)

Earth The planet on which we live. It is third in order from the sun. (p. 17)

effort A force; a push or a pull. (p. 154)

energy The ability to do work. (p. 7)

erosion The movement of rocks and soil by wind or water. (p. 47)

evaporate To change from a liquid to a gas. (p. 13)

fever A higher than usual body temperature; a symptom. (p. 108)

force The push, pull, or lift on an object. Force is needed to do work. (p. 154)

fossils The prints or remains of plants or animals that lived long ago. (p. 58)

friction The resistance to rubbing one object over another; produces heat. (p. 165)

fulcrum The point on which a lever turns. (p. 154)

fungi Plants that are not green. Fungi do not have roots, stems, leaves, or flowers. (p. 91)

gas One of the states of matter. Gases are invisible and do not have a fixed size or shape. (p. 133)

germs A name for bacteria and viruses that cause disease. (p. 109)

glacier A large mass of ice that moves over the land. (p. 52)

grain The seeds of different grasses that are used for food. (p. 82)

granite One kind of igneous rock; forms when melted rock hardens underground. (p. 44)

gravitational attraction Force of attraction between the earth and objects on it. Also, the force that attracts objects to the earth. (p. 16)

groundwater Water below the earth's surface. (p. 49)

Halley's comet Famous comet that nears the earth about every 76 years. (p. 21)

herbivores Animals that eat only plants. (p. 81)

herds Groups of animals that eat mostly plants. (p. 180)

humus Material in soil, formed from decayed plants and animals. (p. 61)

igneous rocks Rocks formed when melted rocks harden. (p. 57)

immunized Having had "shots" to prevent a disease. (p. 111)

inclined plane Any ramp or slope; a simple machine. (p. 156)

irrigation Watering crops when there is not enough rain. (p. 76)

joule A newton meter. (p. 161)

Jupiter A major planet; the fifth planet in order from the sun. (p. 19)

kilometer A metric unit of distance; 1000 meters. (p. 24)

lava Melted rock that flows from a volcano. (p. 44)

lever A simple machine that turns on a point called a fulcrum. (p. 154)

limestone A sedimentary rock formed from bones and shells of sea animals. (p. 57)

liquid One of the states of matter. Liquids have no fixed shape. (p. 133)

liter A metric unit of capacity or volume; 1000 milliliters. (p. 197)

loam Soil made from a mixture of sand, clay, and humus. (p. 60)

lubrication The coating of a surface with a material to cut down friction. (p. 167)

machine Anything that helps people do work. (p. 153)

magma Melted rock deep in the earth. (p. 44)

major planets The large outer planets; Jupiter, Saturn, Uranus, and Neptune. (p. 19)

mantle The part of the earth between the crust and the core. (p. 42)

Mars One of the nine planets. It is fourth in order from the sun. (p. 18)

matter Anything that has weight and takes up space. (p. 131)

Mercury   One of the nine planets. It is first in order from the sun. (p. 16)

metamorphic rocks   Rocks that have been changed by heat and pressure. (p. 59)

meteorite   A meteor that hits the earth. (p. 23)

meteors   Matter from outer space that burns as it enters the earth's atmosphere. (p. 23)

meter   A metric unit of length. (p. 24)

meterstick   A measuring stick, one meter long. (p. 24)

mildew   A kind of fungi that often grows in moist places. (p. 95)

minerals   Chemicals found in and on the earth. Some are needed for growth and health. (p. 115)

moist   Slightly wet; damp. (p. 95)

molecules   The smallest particles of a substance that are like the substance. (p. 142)

nectar   A sweet liquid in the flowers of plants. Bees make honey from it. (p. 184)

Neptune   A major planet; usually the eighth planet in order from the sun. From 1979 to 1998 it will be the ninth planet. (p. 19)

newton   A unit of force in the metric system. (p. 161)

nutrients   The materials the human body needs for growth. (p. 113)

orbits   Plants in which the planets travel around the sun. (p. 15)

packs   Groups of hunting animals. (p. 180)

penicillin   Drug that comes from mold. (p. 91)

physical change   A change in the size, shape, or state of a substance. (p. 141)

pivots   Turns on a point. (p. 154)

planetoids   Planetlike objects between Mars and Jupiter. (p. 20)

planets   The heavenly bodies that revolve around the sun. (p. 7)

Pluto   One of the nine planets; usually the farthest planet from the sun. (p. 19)

pollen   Tiny particles in plant flowers that help produce seeds. (p. 184)

protective coloration   Color pattern that lets an animal blend into its surroundings. (p. 193)

protein   A nutrient the human body needs for growth. (p. 114)

ptarmigan A quaillike bird that lives in cold climates. (p. 195)

pulley A simple machine made up of a wheel with a rope, a belt, or a chain moving over it. (p. 158)

quartz A glassy mineral found in many rocks. (p. 56)

radiant energy Energy that travels through space as waves. (p. 11)

resistance Object moved by a machine; the load. (p. 154)

revolves Moves around. The earth *revolves* around the sun. (p. 29)

rotation Spinning, or turning, on an axis. (p. 29)

sand Loosely packed soil that does not hold water very well. (p. 60)

sandstone A sedimentary rock. (p. 57)

sap A liquid in plants. (p. 86)

Saturn A major planet; the sixth planet in order from the sun. (p. 19)

screw A simple machine. It is an inclined plane twisted into a spiral. (p. 156)

sediment Mud, sand, and other materials that settle out of water. (p. 44)

sedimentary rock Rock made from mud, sand, and pebbles that have been squeezed and cemented together. (p. 45)

simple machines The six machines from which all others are made: lever, inclined plane, wedge, screw, wheel and axle, and pulley. (p. 153)

social insects Insects that live in colonies, such as ants and bees. (p. 184)

solar system The sun and all of the bodies that revolve around the sun. (p. 7)

solid One of the states of matter. Solids have a definite size and shape. (p. 133)

spores Tiny cells, produced by some plants, that may grow into new plants. (p. 94)

states The forms of matter: solid, liquid, and gas. (p. 133)

symptom A sign of sickness or disease. Fever is a symptom. (p. 108)

temperature How hot or cold something is. (p. 11)

territory An area an animal marks off for its own home. (p. 197)

thermometer An instrument that measures temperature. (p. 11)

topsoil Top layer of soil; the best soil for growing things. (p. 61)

Uranus A major planet; the seventh planet in order from the sun. (p. 19)

Venus One of the nine planets. It is second in order from the sun. (p. 17)

viruses Small nonliving things that cause disease. (p. 109)

vitamins A group of chemicals needed for growth and health. (p. 114)

volcanoes Mountains made from cooled lava. (p. 44)

water vapor Water in the form of a gas. (p. 138)

weathering The breaking up of rocks by wind or water. (p. 47)

wedge A simple machine made of two inclined planes joined to form a sharp edge. (p. 156)

wheel and axle A simple machine made of a wheel that turns on a center post, or axle. (p. 158)

work Force moving through a distance. (p. 151)

INDEX